CONNECT
Through THINK FEEL KNOW

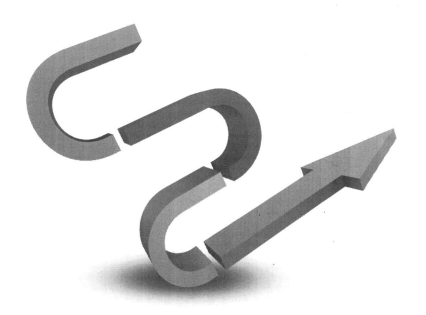

CLIVE HYLAND

Connect through Think, Feel, Know

First published in 2013 by

Anoma Press
48 St Vincent Drive, St Albans, Herts, AL1 5SJ, UK

info@anomapress.com
www.anomapress.com

Book layout by Neil Coe.

Printed on acid-free paper from managed forests. This book is printed on demand to fulfill orders, so no copies will be remaindered or pulped.

ISBN 978-1-908746-75-7

Dedications

For: Christopher and Celeste

Suzy

Tash

Sally

Scott

Tara and Kris

Jacob

Louie

Testimonials

"The corporate world is saturated with management theories, so it is refreshing to come across a book that offers something completely different yet feels like a discovery that you can't believe hasn't been made before. Backed up by science and real application it just makes sense. Adoption into an organizational context requires no deliberation. The Think Feel Know model resonates powerfully with all of us who have people at the heart of our business, believe in people and want to make the most of our people. The most complex machines on the planet suddenly explained: how good is that?"

—Debbie Jones, senior vice president, corporate development, Inmarsat plc – the world's leading satellite communications business

"Like many business people I am acutely aware of how dependent our business is on making the most of our people talent. The Think Feel Know model has the power to engage us all from established leaders to those just starting out on their careers. Old hierarchical approaches to management no longer work. This book offers exciting alternatives for the future."

—Matt Phelan, director 4Ps Marketing

"This wonderfully paced book is packed with extraordinary insight into the ultimately doomed organizational design of big corporations in the early 21st century. My experience of impotence of leaders in business in handling emotion is completely and so reassuringly explained by Clive Hyland. His passionate urgent call for archaic 'immoral' culture of 'measure, measure, measure' to change is a dialog opened decisively in this great book. And my next consulting engagement paraphrasing President Reagan will start with 'Mr CEO, rip down those values statements'. It dissects the myth of pursuing 'an entrepreneurial culture' sought so enthusiastically by corporate west. One of the reasons I love consulting so much is there are pockets of wonderfully inspired corporate executives who get this powerful understanding that they have to change – you have put this argument so convincingly to paper; thank you. The brilliant analogy of the interaction between the three layers of the brain, and the fascinating externalization of our own heartbeat is so cool it hurts. I read this book with so much excitement, my adrenalin levels are still raised days later."

—Dr Adam Poole, ex-surgeon, ex-principal consultant, and entrepreneur

Acknowledgments

To all of my clients and colleagues who have helped me shape this story.

Allan

Adam

Foreword

After starting my business career in financial trading I became quickly aware that understanding people is the key to understanding business success. I then, with my trusted colleagues, set about building a global coaching business that now operates in many countries across the world. Part of this journey was the development of the Think Feel Know model.

The model itself has always aimed to bring a fresh insight to our understanding of human behavior and to do so by using simple language that we can all understand. Clive and I started to share this journey when we first met in 2006 and continued when he joined our business in 2007. What Clive has done since then is take the model to new and inspiring depths of understanding. Our early design of the model had to be intuitive; now, as this book demonstrates, the emerging neurosciences are validating our thinking.

The scope of the book should be an essential read for all people in business, and beyond, who are looking for new ways to develop human potential. It strikes at the heart of leadership, motivation and relationships and challenges the stale approach still relied upon in so many corporate organizations. As new generations of leaders emerge they will do wisely to heed these insights.

Unravelling the science can be a daunting task and Clive has done us a huge favor by capturing some of the key principles in such an engaging and accessible manner. He brings a unique blend of impressive business leadership experience and scientific research to this subject matter and offers us a perspective that is easy to read and energizing to follow.

Occupational psychology had a significant affect on management theory in the 20th century, yet the stresses and strains of modern business organizations provide ample evidence that they are no longer working. In particular, the part we have failed to unlock has been the real potential of the people who sit at the middle of all this. The next decades of this century will look instead to the greater tangibility of neuroscientific data. This book is a great place to start that journey.

Darren Shirlaw, Founder, Navitas (Oct 2012)

Contents

Section I:

A matter of personal importance

"Everyone stumbles over the truth from time to time, but most people pick themselves up and hurry off as though nothing ever happened."

—Winston Churchill (1874-1965)

From a very early age I have been fascinated by what makes people tick and what makes them perform. I remember observing my classmates and how they interacted with one another and thinking even then how intriguing people are. This fascination has stayed with me throughout my life, through my years of study, throughout my 30-year business career and, more recently, in my last seven years as a personal and business coach.

Yet, despite the many years of experience, probably the biggest breakthrough in my understanding of human behavior has only come to me since 2005. The source of this breakthrough? Neuroscience.

After many years of following psychology, my understanding reached a new level when I became exposed for the first time to the emerging research around the function of the human brain and its wider neurological system. For me, the light bulb really went on, and I felt able to put together the pieces of understanding that hitherto had fitted together uncomfortably, like attempting to put together a jigsaw without being able to see the total picture. Now, what was emerging was a real sense of the picture on the box, of how each part relates to the whole.

So my intention in this book is to share this understanding with you and hopefully to give you the chance to reflect, agree or disagree, and, most important of all, take the bits that work for you and help to enrich your experience of business and of life. My aim is that these insights should be applicable across a wide spectrum of life experiences, from close personal relationships, to running a business or building a career, to excelling in the sporting environment, to breaking through the prejudices and limitations of our own thinking and the thinking of those around us. My proposition is that we have so much more to offer ourselves and that the source of this opportunity sits in self-education around how our mind and body really work.

Recent years have provided me with an amazing opportunity to explore the 'science' of human behavior and to examine some of the data available from the most recent research. To be clear, I am no neuroscientist, and I do not have any wish to be a practicing psychologist. The value I aim to bring here is the translation of what I have discovered to be fundamentally important principles of human behavior into everyday life. The study of academics deserves total respect, and I am hugely indebted to them for inspiring me. Yet, my belief is that the principles I will cover in this book are largely misunderstood in the everyday world of Mr Normal. My challenge is to help address this great missed opportunity for so many people and to play my own small part in moving popular understanding of neuroscience to an enjoyable, productive and inspiring level. I will do this by using the Think Feel Know model as a simple yet powerful way of understanding our brains. In particular, I have run my own lens of business and people experience over the scientific principles covered in the book. I sit between the research and rigor of the academic specialist and the interested consumer: I aim to translate their insights into our everyday life experiences.

I will begin this by explaining the basic principles of neuroscience as I understand them. I will refer to the wider sources of some of my reading and research, but it is a list that will be kept simple and short. I would regard it as a great success if some of you felt your appetites whetted and went on to directly study the science in more depth. That would be brilliant. I am trying here to act as the gateway to some of this understanding. We are not all motivated to dig into scientific material ourselves, but some of us are happy to work out our own interpretation of such data and present the basics to a wider audience.

On the other hand, I feel that labeling this book solely as one about the science of human behavior would be inappropriate. Perhaps one day science will be able to explain it all: today it cannot. And to limit our exploration to that which can be scientifically proven would be a gross barrier to the information that is already available to us. So I actively encourage you to use your life experience in interpreting this material. I aim to offer you a rich mixture of the objectivity of science and the subjectivity of art. I ask you to be intuitive in your responses (intuition being one of the subject areas I will cover later). Here this really means testing it out yourself. I believe your own reflections and insights will give you most of the evidence you need. In the last seven years, I have talked this subject matter through many times with colleagues, specialists and clients. I never encounter resistance. People consistently connect with the subject matter on an intuitive level and find it incredibly valuable in making sense of the world they have created around them. I trust you will be able to do the same.

You will see me put forward the proposition that many people connect with stories more than facts. Of course there is a balance to be struck if we are to avoid delusion or fantasy. So, while I will cover some basic scientific principles to help create a credible foundation for our dialog, I will also use stories that will come primarily from my clients (with anonymity preserved, of course) as I give you real-life experiences showing how the principles covered in the book can be applied in everyday reality. On a very few occasions I will draw examples from my own life, as it is the most accessible source of data I have. When I do so I hope you will be able to make that same connection with your own experiences and be able to pull out the parallels. Then we are really sharing the journey.

Another really important theme is language. I intend to use simple language wherever I can. Inevitably this will mean that I will occasionally sacrifice clinical precision and some rigor, but the last thing I want to do is use language that causes people to disconnect because it is too labored or esoteric. My goal is to connect the amazing power of neuroscientific research to the everyday. Of necessity, this means using everyday language. This is, of course, where I may have an advantage over those truly qualified in their fields of research. Their language has to be precise in an arena where they will face critical peer judgment. They cannot take up the challenge of scientific discipline and then set it aside when it suits them. Without their research I would have nothing to say. But I will do my very best to communicate complex subject matter in language that a much wider audience can find engaging. For me the success of this book will be judged by the number of people who read it and feel a sense of connection to my interpretation of the world that surrounds them. Whether you take these insights at face value, or choose to go on with greater scientific reading of your own, is your choice and either is good by me.

It took a very long time for me to discover what has been really driving me in my life, that which you may call my *life-purpose*, and I am not sure yet whether it has always been the same driver or if it has changed with life experience. Whatever your life-purpose, I will try to support you to take a step towards true discovery of who you are today and how you have created your own reality. I believe this has the potential to offer back to you the choices by which you run your life. I say 'offer back' because the choices have always been there; we have just not been able to see them. Should you wish it, your life could change immediately and forever.

This content of this book is inevitably biased towards people in business, as this is where I have spent a great deal of my life.

Yet, the key word here is *people*, not business: its relevance is not limited to the business environment. The central theme is people and what makes us tick. This theme transcends business boundaries and translates into all areas of life, especially relationships. The principles are just as relevant in education, sport, families and communities of all kinds.

I will give some scientific basis to any encouragement I offer, and I will do so in the hope that I enrich the choices available to you. By understanding some of the mechanisms of our bodies, physical and non-physical, we have a chance to take back some choices we may previously have considered unavailable to us. We cannot control what happens to us in life, but we can do a lot to choose our response. This is precisely where I will try to offer you valuable insights that are immediately applicable in your world should you make the choice to move forward with them.

Section II:

Discovering neuroscience

A model for understanding the brain

"Make the most of yourself, for that is all there is of you."

—Ralph Waldo Emerson,
essayist, lecturer and poet (1803-1882)

If we want to truly understand human behavior there is no better place to start than our brains. What I want to do here is present you with a model of the brain to assist in your understanding of human behavior and performance. It cannot be taken literally, as we are dealing with a vastly complex and wonderful 'machine' that even the most dedicated of neuroscientists are only just beginning to understand. Future years will, no doubt, tell us more and more in what should be an amazing journey of discovery into our true potential. Nevertheless, what we can use now is some of the rich source of research and clinical data collected since the millennium.

Central to this has been the emergence of fMRI (functional magnetic resonance imaging) technology that has enabled us to directly monitor live brain activity in a depth previously unavailable. The result, so far, of this decade of clinical research and practice is an emerging picture of the human neurological system that offers important insight into the principles underpinning human behavior. In discovering some of this learning for myself, I have found it powerful and amazing. For me, it adds a completely new layer to the understanding offered by the classical psychologists of the 20th century. Although they were great thinkers in their own right, 20th-century psychologists only had access to dead brains. Trying to understand people by dissecting dead brains is like trying to understand a cow by slicing up a piece of steak. Much of their theory had to be based on hypotheses and behavioral experimentation. It was essentially an observational model. Now we can directly access the brain and see the immediate correlation between brain activity and behavioral response. This emerging understanding is current, relevant, sometimes radical and moving at a fantastic pace of discovery.

It is not my purpose here to try to cover this research in clinical depth, although I will endeavor to keep complete faith with the principles as I have understood them. I have put together in the appendix a short summary of the books and research from which I have formed my understanding. I am very lucky to have had the benefit of direct access to practicing neurologists who helped me to work through my understanding and helped to ensure that I am not misrepresenting the principles here.

In parallel, I would ask you to do your own research. I am not talking about conducting double-blind social experiments or establishing samples of clinically statistical significance. Thank goodness, we can leave that to the experts. But I am asking you to carefully look back on events in your life with a renewed insight, one that could have been very valuable at the time.

The Think, Feel, Know model

"Live as if you were to die tomorrow.
Learn as if you were to live forever."

—Mohandas Gandhi (1869-1948)

The model I will use here represents the brain as consisting of three regions. This represents the anatomy of the brain at a simple level. The main purpose of the model is to draw out the behavioral implications of brain physiology, that is, to demonstrate how each of these regions influences our everyday behavior.

In keeping with the style and ambition of the book, the brain regions in this model will be represented simply as:

- the Thinking brain
- the Feeling brain, and
- the Knowing brain.

The Thinking brain

"A journey of a thousand miles begins with a single step."

—Laozi, philosopher of ancient China (Zhou Dynasty)

Here we are referring to the cortex, the top layer of gray mass that separates us from the animal kingdom. When people talk about the left and right sides of the brain they are generally referring to the cortex. The other layers of the brain do not divide in such a way.

Thinking in terms of the Think Feel Know model, it is helpful to think of this region of the brain as working primarily on the basis of rational processing. It is the region of the brain where we create the rules for living out our existence. It is about process, structure, systems and logic. This is where we process facts and figures, detailed evidence and complex problem-solving. It is the layer of the brain that compares most directly to computers. It is the world of self-awareness, the place from where we look in on ourselves. It is therefore the place of reflection and self-analysis. Rationality lives here, which is the sequence of rules that we have built to make sense of the world around us. It is a clinical and objective world where we are constantly moderated by the mental rules and structures we have created. Methodology and systematic techniques thrive in this environment. Concepts are created here as patterns of thought that help us to make cognitive sense of what is going on around us. It is largely a cerebral experience.

We can recognize many professions that appear to be dominated by this 'Thinking':

- solicitors, whose role is to interpret evidence against a prescribed set of rules (the Law)

- accountants, who use standard methodology to report the detailed facts of business performance

- medical practitioners, for whom the application of methodological rigor is critical to the development of patient care

- researchers in any sense, since this is the world of collection of evidence against a given set of rules and experimentation techniques.

So, when we operate in 'Think' we are at our most clinical and objective. You can spot the signs of somebody in Think behavior: they may have a furrowed brow as they process data; their eyes will typically go up as if they are directly connecting with the cortex; they are looking, but they are not registering anything in particular, almost gazing. This is because the prime energetic focus of the brain at the time is internal processing, and the brain is therefore less tuned to data outside the body. Others may experience this as appearing to be cold and methodical. Their demeanor will be deliberate, measured and workman-like, and their energy will be neutral, neither excited nor anxious. This is the sphere of evidence, analysis, problem-solving and planning.

For most of us, this model representation of the cortex will be relatively easy to grasp. Most people will readily recognize the Thinking layer. Our schooling system has drummed this into our heads. In school we are taught primarily to process and capture information. The teacher tells us how it is. We listen, process, memorize and play back in examinations, to be tested against a prescribed set of criteria. Business environments, particularly in the larger corporate world, also tend to be dominated by 'Think', that is facts and figures, rules and processes, structures and standards. Both share a preoccupation with results. Results are evidence, evidence is data and this type of data is the domain of the Thinking brain.

The Feeling brain

"The heart has reasons which reason cannot understand."

—Blaise Pascal (1623-1662)

Next, we move to the middle layer of the brain, known as the limbic layer, sometimes referred to as 'the mammalian brain' because its primary evolution was developed in mammals.

Here we have a greater challenge. We easily recognized the schooling system above as an example of a Think environment. Not much room for feelings in the examination process. Yet exams can be a very pressurized and stressful experience, which is of course nothing to do with logic. So why do our anxieties get in the way of our ability to remain focused and to concentrate? Why aren't we able to respond to a clinical process in a clinical way? The answer lies in the workings of this 'Feeling' region of the brain.

The Feeling area of the brain works on completely different principles to the Thinking brain. It is where we experience pain, distress, excitement, happiness, fear and anxiety. It is from here that we offer others empathy, confrontation, care and personal challenge. It is from this place that we connect or disconnect with others. The energy of the Thinking layer is neutral, workman-like and channeled. The energy of the feeling layer is potentially volatile, one minute up and the next minute down; it is the realm of excitement and fear, optimism and depression, motivation and resignation, conquest and defeat.

In this place logic and the prescriptive rules of the cortex do not exist. It is a more mysterious place where there is much still to be discovered. It is the place where the brain is most immediately connected to the senses and to the heart. This is the world of energetic connection. Activity triggered here means the body is engaged: no longer the clinical world of the Thinking layer. No longer sitting on the side of the pool observing the techniques of swimming: now we are in the water. Maybe just a toe at first, maybe experiencing the joy of floating on the surface, or maybe feeling overwhelmed like a sense of drowning. It is the world of feelings and emotions.

This Feeling layer of the brain relies more on the senses than it does logic. It picks up energetic signals instantly and sends triggers to the parts of the body that can respond quickest to both opportunity and threat. It is connection to the outside world that is critical here, more than that of internal processing.

And this capability is with us from the point of birth. When a baby is born he or she has negligible thinking ability: this will come quickly but later. The baby will, however, have an energetic capacity to connect with others, which can typically begin with crying immediately after his or her birth. It is hard to deny the immediate energetic connection we feel when a baby cries. Our reaction may be positive or negative, but it is very difficult to ignore. A baby's or a child's crying is for me a great example of nature fine-tuning its ability to attract attention without the use of thought or language. Babies are natural experts when it comes to energetic communication.

Likewise, consider animals, the true developers of the limbic layer. They have no language to call upon and have received no conscious instruction in acceptable behavior, but it is very rare for an animal to not know where it stands in relation to its immediate community. The combination of noises, tone, body position, movement, touch and raw energy transmission or submission can offer us some valuable lessons in avoiding misunderstanding. Animals are rarely confused when it comes to social interaction with their own kind.

Let's explore some of the key features of the limbic region further.

Energy

"The best effect of fine persons is felt after we have left their presence."

—Ralph Waldo Emerson, essayist, lecturer and poet (1803-1882)

To really understand this area of the brain we have to move away from logic and turn instead to the subject of energy. I want to demystify our understanding of emotions. We all experience them every day of our lives. It is what separates us from robots. Yet so often we do not understand them. Frequently, they appear to take us over. We don't know where they come from. We try to control them but sometimes feel they are controlling us. We know there are times when they engulf us and when rationality flies out of the window: powerful, scary and mysterious.

So what is an emotion? I would like to work with the definition that an emotion is *an energetic reaction in the body*. It could be described as a biochemical and electro-magnetic reaction. Think of the language *e-motion*. It is the motion of energy through the body. We often refer to people's *chemistry*, another insight offered by the language that we have so often overlooked. It is our energetic reaction to someone or something, and our biochemistry sits at the heart of this reaction. Hormones are the chemical messengers of the body and are released by our glands to trigger (among other things) an energetic response to our environment.

The role of energy is not confined to the internal response within our bodies. In fact, there is also a direct energetic transaction going on when we interact with others. We trade on energy. People can give us energy (energize us) or they can take it away (drain us). It is not an exchange that is driven by the Thinking brain. The cortex tries to make sense of it after the initial connection or disconnection has taken place, but it cannot have an advance on it. It is the world where we are personally engaged, sometimes apparently without any conscious choice. We just find ourselves there and reacting.

Think of situations when you have walked into a room of people and you have instantly sensed that there is something wrong. A particular dilemma or mess is not obvious, and nobody has said that there is a problem, but you are picking up signals that suggest trouble. This is where you are engaging your limbic brain. Yes, you will pick up logical evidence also, but the point is that the limbic layer clicks in first and starts to assess the situation even before the Thinking brain has got up to speed.

Energy does not obey the rules of human convenience. It exists in its own form and cannot be destroyed. It can only be channeled. It is at this most basic level that we share our molecular structure completely with the universe of which we are a part. Recent scientific development has helped us to understand that we are essentially energetic beings at our very cores.

Those familiar with modern science will understand that much experimentation has been undertaken to research the most basic levels of human existence. Understanding this most fundamental level of our molecular structure is critical to our scientific advancement. When these basic components of our structure are broken down to the smallest possible level, we discover that all that exists is energy. The implications of this are huge. From this has developed the thinking that all forms of existence as we know it are energy-based structures that have taken on varying levels of density: the lower the energy vibration level, the denser the formation. Density leads to material form, whether human or non-human. Rather than space and material form being understood as separate worlds, they now become viewed as belonging to one continuum, the continuum of the universe.

This seems like a strange departure for a book that is essentially about what drives human behavior, but actually it is not. It holds the key to enabling us to begin to understand the realms of energy that underpin our life experience. Much of it appears to defy common logic, but it is probably more accurate to say that it illustrates the limitations of our logical capability so far. To understand energy in a meaningful way, you have to feel it. Thinking alone is not enough. We cannot think our way to sensitivity. Thinking means focusing our energy more on internal processing. Feeling energy is about engaging the senses of sight, sound, smell, touch and taste, and the more mysterious 'sixth sense' we all possess of using our invisible antennae to pick up energetic signals around us.

We now understand that our hearts emit a regular electro-magnetic signal of about 5ft (1.5m) outside our physical bodies. This can be directly evidenced in laboratory conditions. You may have experienced this directly. Some people's energy disturbs us; other people's energy attracts us. Some appear to have a natural gravitas: we need only to sit close to them to feel their energy. Similarly, sexual energy follows the same principles: when we connect sexually it is a very deep sensation. Equally, as a coach, it is critical that I maintain calm energy when I am dealing with clients. There are a number of occasions when I have no need to look at them directly (for instance, when I am writing down conversational notes), yet I will still immediately feel the shift in energy in their bodies when their emotions change. By staying energetically 'clean' myself I am open to receiving their energetic transmissions.

The cortex does not 'get' this: it does not 'do' energy. It is like our hearts being plugged into their own mobile network, but the cortex does not have the password.

Survival

"Think of all the beauty still left around you and be happy."

—Anne Frank (1929-1945)

One of the key scientific breakthroughs in defining our understanding of the importance of the limbic region of the brain was the work of Joseph LeDoux in 1999. His work produced compelling evidence that the physiological connection between the limbic layer and the heart is quicker than the connection between the cortex and the heart. The implications of this are enormous. Essentially, it means that in certain circumstances we react energetically (emotionally) first, and then the rational response comes afterwards. These circumstances are entirely related to our deepest instinct, which is one of survival, and this instinct is never far below the surface.

The ultimate concern of the brain is survival. We will discuss our instinctive response to threats later, but for now we need to understand that the Feeling region of the brain acts as the first guardian against any perceived threat to our survival. It uses data from our senses as radar to spot danger on the horizon. In survival terms it therefore makes absolute sense that it is given the fastest access to the parts of the body that can remove us from threat. When we are in immediate danger we cannot afford to waste time analyzing a threat. We need to clear out all cognitive clutter and make an instantaneous decision. If we are about to be run over by a bus it is not useful to process what bus number it is, we need our legs to move to get out of its way.

The limbic region of the brain, the heart and the autonomic nervous system combine to activate the body. Adrenalin is released and we become primed for action. In all of this, the cortex is left trailing, even if only by mili-seconds, but this is still very significant. It explains, for instance, why footballers concede to the 'red mist' in a moment of anger and kick out at an opponent who has threatened them. If the cortex were in control the rational brain would have prevented this reaction, but it is not. All it can do is catch up after the event, all too often after the damage has been done and the referee's red card has been produced.

Likewise, the Feeling layer can take over when we sense immediate opportunity. Here we are dealing with the same chain reaction as that of threat, but the association is now positive. Most of us have experienced times when we 'got carried away' with the excitement of a moment. After risking life and limb (or at least our social standing) we are left afterwards with the question, "Why the hell did I do that?"

We must remember that the limbic layer of our brain was with our ancestors long before the cortex became fully developed. Interpretations vary, but it is safe to say that Homo sapiens have been around for some 100,000 years. Most of this has been spent in the harsh environment and high physical threat of Stone Age times. Humans did not then have the capability of advanced reasoning that would come later. Their survival depended in part on their ability to sense their environment and to do so quickly. This is exactly how the Feeling layer operates.

The brain cannot cope with treating the complete mass of data it absorbs every second of the day as new data. Take any scene on any day and much of the experience that surrounds us will not even be registered in our conscious awareness. To try to process all data through the cortex would render us slow and ponderous in terms of decision-making and would require enormous memory capacity for little apparent value. We cannot operate this way when it comes to sensing threat. So it sets up matching mechanisms from birth that help us to build a memorized picture of the data that really matters, especially that which is critical to our survival.

A key device in the brain in this survival process is the amygdala. The amygdala operates as a single system, although it actually consists of a pair of walnut-shaped units that sit in the region of the brain behind the eyes. A key part of its physiological role is to look for survival risks. It operates like radar and looks for signs of danger. It does this by rapidly checking what it 'sees' and comparing this with previously recorded experiences. If it spots a match it collaborates with the hippocampus, which can be thought of here as the filing cabinet of the memory network. Together they retrieve the 'file' and check out the previous experience. If this suggests danger by recalling that the recorded experience resulted in negative personal impact, it will fire off the alarm system in the body. This results in a chain reaction via the autonomic nervous system, which releases adrenalin into the body and primes it for action – the flight or fight response. I will deal with this subject in more depth later, but the point to register now is that when it comes to feelings it is no longer just cerebral – the whole body is engaged, and, crucially, the reaction is triggered faster than the speed of rational thought.

You may be walking along a pavement and the fact that a passerby sneezes is hardly important enough to commit to memory and is superfluous to the situation you are facing. Yet at the same time you may not have become immediately consciously aware that an oncoming bus is driving very close to the kerb. If you do not very quickly recognize the danger signals of the wayward bus your survival is jeopardized. The amygdala is the device that will trigger the body to react to the danger. By using our senses it responds immediately to our environment. It cannot wait for the cortex to analyze the data. It reacts first; the questions come later.

Stories

"There are no rules of architecture
for a castle in the clouds."

—GK Chesterton, English writer (1874-1936)

It has been explained above that this limbic region of the brain operates by creating and spotting patterns. It is always on the lookout for associative connections. It is this associative tendency that provides the fertile ground for linking experiences through stories. Facts are unimportant here, as is the application of prescribed methodology. Its search for patterns leads it to naturally create connections between pieces of data and to follow the trail of meaning. This world is not one of precision; it is one of approximation. As speed is the essence, 'close enough' will do. It is a world of action and reaction, not analysis. It is about engagement or retreat, not sitting on the fence.

Consider the best story-tellers: it is not the precision of their language that engages you; it is their energy, the tonality of their voice, the intonation and the skilled use of silence.

Tonality is itself an energetic pattern applied in language. We have all experienced how difficult it is to listen intently to someone who speaks monotonously. This has nothing to do with the message. Neutral energy is perfect for the cortex but not for the limbic layer. Without energetic connection we will not give the deliverer of the message access to our engagement. The story-teller has to create an experience. So does any other person who wants to get his or her message across. The associative reaction of the limbic region will create an internal image and generate the feelings that go with it. If the limbic layer is engaged then the cortex will follow.

A fascinating insight into this can be drawn from our experience of dreaming. We dream every night and in regular patterns throughout the night. Yet we are only aware of these dreams when we wake up in the middle of one. Let's look at this neurologically. When we sleep it is time for the cortex to have a break. The cortex is the guardian of our rules and moderates the behavior of the 'unruly' limbic layer. When the cortex rests, the limbic layer has the opportunity to flow free without constraint. What is a dream other than a sequential association of non-related facts? There is no logic involved, just the limbic magician playing its game of patterns. I am sure we have all experienced dreams where we start off in one scene and end up in a totally non-related one as we wake, like the work of an author who has dropped all his pages and put them back together with no sense or reason. At the point of awaking the cortex becomes re-engaged. It brings the dream to an end, sometimes because the experience is going too far and creating a fear response in the body (a nightmare) or because it has 'heard' an unfamiliar noise from the outside world that has set the alarm bells ringing. The cortex has resumed its role of everyday moderation, but it is never really in absolute control.

A similar example is when we consume too much alcohol. In this case, the cortex goes into involuntary standby. The physiological effect of the alcohol is to reduce the influence of the cortex and for the limbic layer this means *party time*. Without the constraints of the neurological moderator, the feeling layer can now go where it wants, which can mean excitement, fun and devil-may-care, or it can mean sinking into anger, self-pity and depression. In fact, it can quite easily achieve both ups and downs all within the timescale of one evening. We can all testify to the acquaintance who has gone too far in the pursuit of immediate euphoria only to come tumbling down to earth very quickly afterwards.

Creativity

"I will love the light for it shows me the way; yet I will love the darkness for it shows me the stars."

—Augustine 'Og' Mandino II, American author (1923-1996)

It is important to recognise that the limbic layer also holds the key to our creativity. Unlike the rules and structure of the thinking layer, here we are in the free-flowing world of energy. Energy will not recognize rules, and it does not sit in cognitive boxes. Thinking belongs to science: Feeling belongs to art. This is the difference between deductive reasoning that starts wide and breaks down into rational component parts, and creative ideas that start from nothing and expand.

It is not that the limbic layer operates in isolation, it actually collaborates with the cortex in the development of the idea, but the essential creative spark comes from the limbic source, from its ability to operate associatively and tangentially. It is lateral rather than linear processing. It is the world of the artist and the musician. After all, what is music at its most basic level other than a rhythmic beat overlaid (lyrically or associatively) by a story? The combined effect of energetic connection and story-telling goes a long way to explain why music has the power to 'touch our souls'. Similarly, painters will tell you that it is the subjective experience of the art form that matters most. They lay no claim to objectivity. They offer their form of expression as something that we can share in whatever way we choose. Imagine the scientist working that way.

Consider for a moment the creative geniuses who have enriched our art, our learning and our history, from Mozart to van Gogh. Reflect on how many of these people have been regarded as eccentrics or perhaps even social misfits. In physiological terms there is a reason for this. In these people the driving force in their behavior is usually this Feeling region. When passion or creativity is aroused, it engulfs the moderating influence of the cortex. The cortex is the place where the rules of social engagement abide. This is where we temper our first reactions and consider our language and behavior before we express ourselves. The world would be a very different place if we really just said what we felt. But in these people these rules are secondary. What does social appearance or etiquette matter when you have an idea that could change the world, when you have discovered a breakthrough in your art or science? So it is hardly surprising that our creative geniuses may appear as unconventional; they are. They fight the limitations of convention and use associative thought and energy to break through these rules.

So, in everyday life, the professions and vocations we associate with the Feeling region of the brain will be carers, nurses and social workers, whose capacity for empathy creates connections with their clients; artists and musicians, who express their passion through their art forms; and media and design people, who are in the world of creative presentation and artful connection. They are the people who bring warmth and excitement to our lives.

This then is the world of Feel in our model representing the limbic region of the brain, the rich tapestry of associative exploration, feeling, energy and creativity. This is where our experience of life is felt most acutely and dramatically.

So, if the cortex is driven by rationality and the limbic region driven by energy, what of the third and final region of the model?

The Knowing brain

"Greatness lies not in being strong, but in the right use of strength."

—Henry Ward Beecher, Congregationalist clergyman (1813-1887)

The base region of the brain is the basal region, sometimes referred to as 'the stem' or 'reptilian brain'. This is the area that sits above the spinal column and is the oldest part of the brain in ancestral terms. Humans developed the cortex and mammals developed the limbic layer, but this layer was there from the very beginning. It represents our deepest past and still holds many secrets. It is the core of our subconscious, where we operate well away from the influence of the cortex. My aim here is not to try to explain exactly how it works (neuroscience is still working on that one) but I can offer some insights into how it influences, and sometimes drives, our behavior.

Instincts

Central to our understanding of this region of the brain is the role of human instincts. Instincts are a bit like feelings in the sense that we know they are an important part of our lives but we appear not to really understand them. In the baby example above, when the baby was born she knew how to use her energetic capability. The baby knew that crying would generate attention and that creating attention was essential to her ability to survive. How did she know? This is because she was told to do so by the instinctive instructions that sit in the basal layer of the brain. In terms of this model, then, instincts are defined as the set of genetic survival instructions that we are born with: the hereditary gift from our parents. Our instincts are the set of genetic programmes passed down to us by our parents and our ancestors. They sit at the very essence of our creation. As instructions they operate at the autonomic level of our physiology, which means they operate automatically without any need for conscious input. In some ways they are better described as pre-conscious in that they already exist before any cognitive or conscious capability is developed. They are central to our deoxyribonucleic acid (DNA) and form the core of our individual genetic footprint that extends throughout every cell in our body.

When it comes to behavior, instincts have a huge affect on how we respond. The survival instinct sits deepest in this region of the brain. We saw the role of the amygdala above: while the amygdala itself sits within the limbic region, it remains an outpost for the basal region and is the first to trigger a reaction to any survival threat. Here it is about speed of response rather than precision. Time is of the essence. And now it is accompanied by a key sense of purpose. The most fundamental instinct of all is the survival of ourselves and those who carry our genes. Now our energy is channeled. Now we are clear about the outcome we are pursuing.

In terms of the model I am using in this book, we are now discussing Knowing behavior. When we are operating in Knowing mode, our instincts have taken over, and we have the answer. This begins with the survival instinct itself so that when it is triggered we know exactly what we need to do to address danger. As we move through life this becomes more elaborate as we interpret the world and decide our place within it. Gradually we develop a sense of our own ambition and what we want to achieve in life. This becomes woven into our instinctive responses and the library of references we have built up at this basal level to guide our behavior. Just as our 'pre-life' (genetics) gave us the early answers, we are now building our own life experiences and the lessons we have learned along the way.

No need for analysis, nor even any need to get excited. When we are in Knowing we know the answer, so let's just get on with it. Therefore, people with a primary Knowing style are seen as decisive, focused and certain. They are experienced by others often as powerful in their self-conviction, although this can also be experienced as arrogance and closed-mindedness. They operate by 'gut instinct' and are usually prepared to back their own 'hunches'. If you want a decision, go to a Knower. It does not mean that he will make the right decision, but he will make one on the basis of his beliefs and experience.

Let's develop this last point. Experience is central to the primary Knowing response. The newborn baby referred to earlier has, of course, no experience of life, so she has to rely on the genetic programming of her parents and ancestors. These instincts at this stage are like a new computer program – one with very little application data. The capability is latent, like a new spreadsheet. It is capable of performing, but it has no application unless it has data to work with. So, from the moment we are born, we start absorbing data, populating the programs that reside in our brain so that they can start to build their own, very personal picture, of the world. As we build these layers of data through experience, we also build our interpretations of what is going on around us and with it our response decisions. This is truly intelligent software that accumulates its capability through life, especially the early stages of life when the pages are blank with plenty of capacity for new data.

In physiological terms, we operate in Knowing mode when the amygdala has spotted a match with our recorded experience. The amygdala recalls the scene and checks with the hippocampus to see what the outcome of this experience was last time. If the result was negative, the autonomic system goes into a fear response, and triggers the motor- neural system to respond immediately to take evasive or aggressive action. However, if the previous recorded experience was positive the brain will believe it already has the answer and will follow its pre-programmed response. Hence the decisive nature of this behavior and the conviction that goes with it.

Neurologists will often refer to heuristics. These are simple rules-of-thumb programmed into the brain to produce these quick and decisive responses. If the answer (program) already exists, why use critical brain power to create a new answer? This is not efficient. So we regularly use what appear as reflex responses to situations we perceive we have experienced before.

So far, this sounds great – the decisive, convinced style that lets us know where we stand and what needs to be done. Unfortunately, that is not the whole story. If it were we would all be clambering to exploit our Knowing style to the maximum. The truth is that, while this style is often seen to be powerful and charismatic, there are also real challenges that come with it.

First, as we get older the pages of our life experience become full, and our ability to stay open-minded becomes more limited. Our experiences of the past can act as our anchor to keep us from drifting, but they can also close us to new ideas and mindsets. When the basal layer takes a primary role in our responses we are typically operating with a closed mind. The second we click into our Knowing we stop listening. We don't need any new data because our mind is made up. This would be more effective if we had really established a very precise match when we evaluated the scene that confronted us; however, the basal layer is not a world of precision. It is the world of immediacy, of taking the primal decisions needed to sustain our survival.

In Stone Age times, when the bear came from behind the bush, we did not have time to be distracted by any data other than that which directly related to our survival. In this mode, the brain becomes much more targeted, that is, it uses all its instincts to focus on the data that matters, and *only* the data that matters. The challenge arises because our matching is based on loose approximation rather than precise depth. In this sense, the brain has memorized images that appear to match with the scene it is now surveying, but it remains an approximation. This means that the comparison we are drawing could be relevant or it could be irrelevant. It explains why we usually feel we are right when we operate instinctively, but it does not necessarily make us right.

Second, because the basal layer operates at the most primal level, it does not do detail. Detailed analysis is something it leaves to the cortex because it requires very high levels of linear processing capacity. The consequence for the primary Knowing style is that the person concerned will not be naturally inclined to check out his initial hunch with any detailed evidence before he commits to his response. Even if he does check it out, he will often interpret such data in a way that simply rationalizes the position he has already taken. And if the Knower does not get his own way, the frequent response will be that of withdrawal and sulking. For the strong Knower, there are only two options – his way or the wrong way. When confronted with facts that even he cannot post-rationalize to justify his original response he either will become confrontational or will withdraw – the modern-day version of flight or flight. When a primary Knower is involved in the game you either play with his ball or he will take his ball home.

Intuition

"Have the courage to follow your heart and intuition. They somehow already know what you truly want to become. Everything else is secondary."

—Steve Jobs, co-founder of Apple Inc (1955-2011)

Operating in Knowing mode means we are responding intuitively. It is interesting that people readily understand the term 'intuition' but usually struggle to explain it. It is an important consideration for this model, so I will offer a personal explanation here. I explained above that instincts can be considered to be the set of genetically programmed instructions we are born with. I also explained that instincts cannot operate in the real world without data. The data we are discussing here is the data of life: how we experience our immediate environment and how we react to it. This starts with the elementary responses of the newborn child and, through life, we will continue to lay down new experiences and to memorize our reactions to those experiences. This combination of instincts and experiential data is what I define as 'intuition': it is the absorption of this data via the limbic system and the processing of this data through to the basal layer of the brain: instincts plus experiential data = intuition.

This is why we often find it difficult to define 'intuition', because it bypasses the cortex. Intuition is not rational. This does not mean that it is irrational or that it is right or wrong. It is just a different intelligence process. It explains sometimes why we find it so difficult to articulate our intuitions or our hunches. We have taken on data at a subconscious level. 'Subconscious' here means the limbic and basal layer, which are collaborating without the immediate assistance of the cortex. Hence, we are often confused ourselves when we have a hunch, for example, about a person or an idea, but we can find no rational evidence to back it up. Most of us will have been in situations where we are meeting somebody for the first time and we experience a conflict between our logical response and our intuitive one. The person we are listening to is saying all the right things and ticking all the logical boxes, but on some level, it does not ring true. We are absorbing other data subconsciously that is telling us something different, be it body language, interpersonal energy or an association at the back of our minds, and this is making us wary.

So, when we are in Knowing mode, the cortex has been largely excluded. Logical rules and linear processing are not required. The limbic system has tuned into all its senses to capture data from both the external world and the internal one and has referred this data to its basal colleague: job done, decision made.

Herein lies one of life's classic dilemmas. Do we trust our instincts and intuitions, knowing that they could be based on approximated data and inappropriate comparisons with our past experiences? Or do we ignore them and the rich source of data available via the totality of our senses? Alternatively, do we stick to the world of hard evidence and objective analysis? There is no simple answer, and in the pages ahead I hope we can at least share a better understanding of what each option offers. For now, my belief is that we do well to heed our instincts as they are a representation of who we really are at our deepest level. Our instincts exist to guide and protect us, particularly when our survival is at risk. On the other hand, we should be alive to their limitations: they serve us best as our guide and not our only master.

Nature v nurture

"No trumpets sound when the important decisions of our life are made. Destiny is made silently."

—Agnes de Mille, American dancer and choreographer (1905-1993)

For me the perspective above also offers us a neat answer to the nature v nurture debate. Are we ultimately driven by our genetic programming or by our experience of life? There is a huge amount of research and commentary available on this. Can the child of the career criminal really rise above her instinctive programming to choose different responses to her environmental and family challenges? Can she really break away and free herself from the learned responses of her parents? If she does 'succeed' where the parent 'failed', is this because she is genetically programmed differently or because she has chosen different responses to her environment? Again, for me, there is no one-sided answer.

In the 'battle' between nature and nurture we have to declare a truce. In fact, there is no battle. They are equally important. They are intense collaborators working towards a common end. The collection and processing of experiential data and the behavioral response to this is a complex interaction between all regions of the brain, and the scientific understanding of this interplay is in its infancy. What a fascinating journey of discovery this will be as our understanding of these subconscious activities in our brain are gradually exposed to us by technological and scientific advances.

Vision, values and beliefs

"Ability is what gives you the opportunity;
belief is what gets you there."

—Apollo

This is the region of the brain where we make reference to our 'rules of life', the guiding principles we have laid down through the lessons taught by our own life experience. Rules of social engagement are generally the domain of the Thinking brain and directly moderate our behavior, but this goes much deeper.

Rules of social engagement help to guide and moderate our behavior, but they rarely help us with how we feel. This is why we so often have to keep a lid on our feelings while we behave in a manner apparently appropriate to the occasion. The content of this book demonstrates that ultimately our emotions are more powerful than our thoughts when it comes to influencing behavior. Thus, any rules of engagement laid down in the Thinking brain will not help us emotionally. For this help we have to look to the real powerhouse – the

Knowing brain. The Knowing brain provides the anchors that guide us: it is not directly concerned with how we behave socially, but it directly influences how we feel.

The brain cannot define a new rule for feelings every time we come across a new situation. Because survival sits at the heart of our emotions, we need to react quickly in the event of threat. Emotions are the body's mechanism for immediate behavioral response, for taking reflexive action. So, emotional rules cannot be made up as we go along. Equally, our pursuit of meaning in life will be extremely challenged if we do not have these emotional anchors to help us make cumulative sense of our journey. Emotions are the essence of our experience of life, and they have to build their own reference library to guide us. These references include vision, values and beliefs.

Popular use of this language often overlaps and can cause misunderstanding. While I cannot claim objective authority on this, I will offer explanations for vision, values and beliefs that are consistent with the overall model for this book.

A vision in this context is an internal visual reference point held in our memory that helps us to guide our direction of travel. It is the lighthouse in the fog. A meaningful vision gives us a channel for our energy. If we can connect with this vision it gives us a sense of purpose. If we can see the lighthouse and if we trust its purpose then we will allow it to guide us. Emotional energy without such a vision is unfocused and bounces unproductively without a meaningful course.

It is the power of a vision that gives an athlete the resilience to continue to commit a large part of her life to the outcome she wants from her sport. This applies over a long period, for example, training through the four-year cycle to ensure peak performance at the time of the Olympics. It also applies in the moment, when the athlete visualizes the immediate outcome she has trained for in her sporting contest. In the same way, a person in business can sustain a high commitment level by connecting with his own personal vision, such as the next step in his career.

At the organizational level, the same principles apply: the creation of a business vision can potentially be very powerful in igniting and aligning the collective energy of the people in the business. However, regrettably, I have to report that, in my experience, this is rarely the case, despite all the effort aimed at achieving this through the plethora of management theories available. Many businesses have a vision, but it only comes alive if the people involved can connect with it. If it does not energize its audience through such a connection, it is simply data: information that can at best provide clarity, but will not motivate.

Our personal values are our point of reference for checking out how we feel about the things in life that really matter to us. They help us to decide right from wrong. They are an emotional and intuitive guide, not directly concerned with behavioral response, although the result is often seen at the behavioral level because of the impact of emotions on behavior. Just as explained in some of the earlier scenarios, we accumulate through life our experiences and our reflections on how we feel about them. Over time we establish a pattern of how we feel about certain emotional stimuli, and we refer back to these patterns to enable a consistency of response. These are the anchors that tell us what we feel is morally right and what is wrong. They are essentially subjective references that provide the rudder for our emotional journey. They sit in the Knowing brain and they directly influence and channel the energy of the Feeling brain. They are our conscience.

Beliefs are more directly associated with our sense of where we fit in the wider picture of life. Our beliefs are our interpretation of the world around us, our personal answers to the most fundamental questions about life itself. Our beliefs are our own view of where our own personal piece of the jigsaw fits into the overall picture.

So, to recap: vision gives us a channel for our energy and a sense of direction; values help us to make emotional and moral sense of the now; and beliefs give us an overriding context of where we fit in the bigger picture, in the universe and in life itself.

Despite recent advances in technology, the Knowing brain remains scientifically elusive and reveals itself very slowly to our mission of discovery. For now, we have to content ourselves with scratching at the surface of the wonderful and mysterious workings of the basal region.

We have recognized the Knowing style as decisive, powerful, fast and certain. We have also acknowledged some of the dangers of overreliance on instincts. Knowers beware. You have a natural power and decisiveness immediately available to you, but it does not necessarily make you right. And, as you go through life building your knowing responses, you are in danger of isolating yourselves from those around you. As a coach of people in powerful leadership positions I always need to have the "Julius Caesar" conversation with my clients, many of whom have a very strong Knowing style. It is this strength of Knowing that helped them to achieve success in their careers, by enabling them to stand out from the crowd. But Knowing overplayed becomes arrogance and a closed mind. In the end unfettered Knowing can become dictatorship, and most dictators end up on the steps like the Roman emperor, with an abundance of knives in their back from so-called 'friends' they have passed along the way.

Now, let's take a further look at examples in everyday life that can help us understand how the layers work together in forming our own particular behavioral styles.

Interaction between the regions

"We must not allow the clock and the calendar to blind us to the fact that each moment of life is a miracle and mystery."

—HG Wells (1866-1946)

Of course, the reality is that the brain works as a total system with constant interaction between the 'regions'. However, understanding the different principles underpinning the activity of these regions can help us start to unravel some of the secrets of human behavior.

Decisions

"A 'no' uttered from the deepest conviction is better than a 'yes' merely uttered to please, or worse, to avoid trouble."

—Mohandas Gandhi (1869-1948)

We can demonstrate this by looking at how we make decisions. The history of research around this area typically regarded to have begun with an incident in 1848 when a railroad construction worker by the name of Phineas Gage suffered an accident involving dynamite. Gage's job was to prepare the area for laying the tracks by using explosives. On this particular occasion he succeeded only in blowing up himself. The offending stick of dynamite penetrated his skull and severed the main connections between the Thinking and Feeling areas of the brain. Remarkably, he survived. Although largely recovering physically and living for another 20 years, he apparently underwent major behavioral change. A previously reliable and dedicated worker, he now became 'dysfunctional' and appeared to lose all 'moral fiber'. In particular, he seemed completely unable to make everyday decisions. He lost his sense of purpose.

I trust that more recent clinical responses would have been less judgmental and more conscious of the effects of trauma but that is not the point here. The point is that this was a real example of a demonstrable link between brain function and human 'personality' or behavior. For the first time, this research was throwing light on the nature of the interaction between the different regions of the brain. In particular, Phineas had lost his ability to make the everyday decisions that give our lives direction and meaning. The basis for decision-making is created when the Thinking and Feeling regions of the brain are aligned. When these regions were unable to effectively communicate, his decision-making capacity was removed. Likewise, he struggled to access effectively his Knowing region where he would normally be able to tap into his sense of identity and purpose. He was still alive, but was he just existing?

As we look back, the implications of this were huge but, unfortunately, the clinicians of the time did not have the technology to exploit this insight. Instead, the analysis of human behavior at that time remained largely in the hands of philosophers and early psychologists. For all their expansive thinking, 20th-century psychologists were also limited by the lack of access to real-time brain data. Dissecting dead brains was a core aspect of clinical discipline and, while valuable in developing our understanding of the anatomy and structure of the brain, a true understanding of the physiology and functionality of the brain by its very nature requires observation of the live brain in action.

So we had to wait almost until the 21st century for the critical scientific breakthroughs made possible through the development of functional MRI scanning technology, which provides us with insights and evidence that the 20th-century psychologists could only have dreamed about.

Learning

"Failure is the key to success; each mistake teaches us something."

—Morihei Ueshiba, founder of the martial art of aikido (1883-1969)

A great example of such interaction between the layers is what happens when we learn to drive. The initial understanding of the requirements of driving and the rules to be followed sits within the functionality of the cortex. This is where we will create new rules by laying down new neural pathways. Next comes the practice of driving, which is the domain of the limbic region. Now all the senses are engaged in the operation of the techniques being learned, executed and mastered. Now the brain is operating like a missile-guidance system where the requirements are known (defined in the cortex) but practice is needed to 'lock on' to the target, to engage the wider senses and the motor-neural system. 'Practice makes perfect' is the principle here, so that we continually refine our operation without rewriting the rules.

Eventually the techniques are sufficiently practiced for us to take the driving test and, hopefully, pass. The difference now is that the solution has been defined, the program has been written. The hard, conscious effort of the learning process is behind us and the rules are known. Within a couple of years of passing our driving test, we find ourselves driving home and not even remembering the journey. Why? It is because the solution is already defined. Why waste the cortex's energy creating new rules when perfectly adequate rules already exist? Just follow them.

In this example, the brain sequence of learning has followed the usual route, which is cortex to limbic to basal (Thinking to Feeling to Knowing). But this isn't always the case.

Survival

"Truth alone will endure, all the rest will be swept away before the tide of time."

—Mohandas Gandhi (1869-1948)

There are times when the limbic and basal layers cut through the mass of information processed by the cortex and bring about an immediate result. This is never as clear as when we are in danger.

Consider the previous example of yourself walking along, taking in your surroundings, when in your wider field of vision you vaguely register that a bus is running the risk of mounting the pavement. In this case, the senses kick in much more quickly than the cortex and the basal response takes over instantaneously, taking the necessary action to remove you from the danger. You are moving away before the cortex has even worked out what is going on.

Confronted by such an immediate and ultimate threat, the physiology of our brain responds and focuses all activity on survival. The oxygenated blood supply in the brain is redirected to the areas that can affect the immediate survival response, often referred to as 'flight or fight'. There is no time for analysis and deliberation: this comes afterwards. There is only time for a response. The immediate after effect of such a 'shock' is often a sense of confusion and a feeling of the heart pumping hard. Confusion is the result of the cortex being in 'catch-up' and needing a little while to piece together what has happened. The heart response is a reflection of the adrenalin rush needed to get your body primed to respond.

I had a recent personal example of this, which is quite everyday by nature but which helped me to understand what goes on in these situations. I had just completed some work with a client team in a London hotel, and I was starting to make my way to the train station. I walked across the frontage of the hotel without noticing that there was a driveway on my left with a car parked in it. As I was walking, I noticed that my shoelace was undone, and I knelt to tie it up. Unbeknown to me, there was a driver in the car and she started to reverse along the driveway. I was in danger, but I had no conscious awareness of it. I had knelt exactly in the blind spot of the car driver where she would have not been able to see me. If I had not reacted, she would undoubtedly have driven over my trailing foot, which was laid out behind me as I was doing my shoelace. Yet somehow I sensed danger. I really had no conscious awareness of what was going on, but I somehow knew I had to move very quickly. I instinctively moved my back foot and was able to get it an inch or two off the ground before I experienced the impact of being hit by the car's rear wheel. The levitation off the ground was just enough to cause my foot to be knocked sideways instead of being crushed.

Somehow, I had avoided the immediate danger, but I needed a few seconds to piece together what had happened. The car had come directly from behind me so I had not seen it. This was a noisy rush hour time in London, so I had not heard it, at least not consciously. The first time I had become aware of anything specific was as I was already raising my foot, and I became vaguely aware of a blur passing behind me. Conscious processing in these circumstances would have been too slow. I was saved from damage by a combination of senses and intuition that recognized the danger and knew what had to be done to protect me and needed no new conscious input to do so.

The latter part of the last century has enabled us to do much to understand the conscious mind (the cortex), but maybe we have been so dominated by this that we have occasionally been inclined to reduce all understanding to that of the logical, that is, to attribute everything to the cortex. Yet, more recent scientific developments are demonstrating more and more the power of the subconscious mind (the limbic and basal layers). It appears to have a crucial and fundamental affect on our behavior, especially at times when we appear to need it the most.

Self-awareness

"We don't see things as they are, we see things as we are."

—Anaïs Nin, French–Cuban author (1903-1977)

Yet, do not be fooled. I have intentionally devoted more time so far to explaining the world of the limbic and basal regions of the brain. This is because I believe they are the least understood. However, it would be a huge mistake to underestimate the power of the cortex in making our behavioral choices. This is the region where we lay down our chosen rules of personal behavior, and core to this is the pre-frontal cortex.

The pre-frontal cortex is the area of the brain where we 'make sense' of who we are. Confronted by the quicker reactions of the limbic and basal regions, the pre-frontal cortex pieces together how this contributes to its sense of self, that is, a self-analysis of the complete experience of who we are. Part of the after effect of experiencing emotion is making sense of what has just happened to us and why we have behaved the way that we have. This is fundamental to any understanding of human behavior and to any prospect of producing behavioral change. Without this 'making sense' activity we have no ongoing basis for modifying our own rules of behavior. We would simply react emotionally and instinctively. The limbic and basal layers operate in real time, in the moment. Reflection and self-analysis is left to the pre-frontal cortex. This is where we decide not only who we think we are but also how we wish to present ourselves to the world.

Research suggests that we do not complete our first comprehensive view of our 'self' until the age of 24. Of course, refinement of this initial view will continue through life, but the completion of adolescence and the immediately following years usually takes us to a place where we have decided who we believe we are and the persona we will adopt when we interact with the outside world. This is a natural part of maturing. However, because we have now chosen our position, we have created a tendency to understand all further experience through these rules of self. This makes us efficient, directed and focused, but it also brings with it the seeds of inflexibility to personal change. It's a catch-22. We need this self-reinforcement to navigate our way through life.

Navigation is useless without understanding the position that we are starting from. Our view of self is essential if we are to avoid meandering through life's emotions without learning. Yet reinforcement of our behavior patterns will by its very nature limit our ability to stay open-minded and flexible in our behavioral responses. The more we reinforce the more intractable we become. Therefore, opening up new ways of learning and self-examination sits at the core of behavioral change. If we simply look at life the way we always have, we will inevitably draw the same conclusions.

It is this self-analysis that separates us from the animal kingdom, this preoccupation with making sense of who we are. Animals appear to be blissfully unaware of this human need and live their lives much more substantially in the moment. Of course, not having access to this capability carries a significant price in terms of animals' ability to accelerate learning and development and to maximize their influence on their environment. On the other hand, with the gift of self-awareness comes the challenge of search for meaning, a journey that can present all the highs of enlightenment and self-fulfilment together with all the lows of confusion and despair.

I will return to this challenge when I look at advanced performance in chapter 4, particularly in relation to effecting personal change.

Behavioral styles

"Where there is an open mind, there will always be a frontier."

Charles F Kettering, American inventor, engineer and businessperson (1876-1958)

So far I have concentrated mainly on giving you some scientific basis for the rest of the book. I now want to start bringing this alive with some simple examples of people's styles and behaviors. At this stage, I will rely on the much simpler language of Thinking, Feeling and Knowing. I will refer to Thinkers, Feelers and Knowers but before doing so, I need to qualify my language.

As already explained, the Thinking, Feeling and Knowing model represents the three regions of the brain – respectively, the cortex, the limbic layer and the basal layer. When I refer to a Thinker, for instance, I am actually referring to somebody whose primary behavioral style is Thinking as described by this model. So in fact I should be saying primary Thinker. Unlike many personality profiling tools, this model rejects the tendency to pigeonhole people. The reality is that we can move between Thinking, Feeling and Knowing styles very rapidly – within seconds in fact. So please do not get the impression that somebody momentarily labeled a Thinker is stuck in this mode for the majority of his or her life. What I mean then is somebody who is in the Thinking state at a particular moment in time.

Each of us will exhibit behavioral tendencies and, when mapped over a longer period, we may well see that we tend to favor one style over the others. This is what the model refers to as the primary style. Alternatively, we may find that two styles tend to dominate or vie for position. Now we refer to the primary and secondary styles. The style we use the least is simply referred to as the other style. Some people will move easily and naturally between all three styles and exhibit no clear pattern: I refer to this as a balanced style.

There are two golden rules that need to be established up front before using this model. First, we use all three styles throughout our lives. Second, no one style is better than the others. Even the term 'balanced' can sound positively judgmental. It does not mean that those exhibiting a more dominant pattern are unbalanced in any judgmental sense; it simply means that they tend to concentrate their energy more around one or two styles. Each style would be seen as having both strengths and weaknesses, opportunities both to connect with and disconnect from people. This will become clearer as the model is explained.

Typically, Thinking behavior will appear as structured and controlled. Primary Thinkers like to think about what they say before they say it and tend to be deliberate in their conversational style. They tend to dress more cautiously or at least to the more predictable requirements of their role or profession. They are happy with logic and detail, and they like clarity and precision. They tend to be seen as reliable and diligent, albeit maybe ponderous. They are more inclined to be clinical and objective.

In behavioral terms, it is usually easy to spot the primary Feelers. They will typically be bubbly, outgoing, engaging and prone to mood swings. They can be creative and challenging. They like to respond in the moment, not being big on plans or sticking to any that have been made. Alternatively, they may express their emotions more passively, for example through empathy and warmth. Some are more inclined to internalize their feelings. Whether expressed or subdued, emotions sit at the heart of their behavior.

Knowers' behavior is all about taking a position: getting to the point. There is no fuss or undue emotionality in the world of Knowing: just do it. Certainty is their trademark. They know what they want and they just go out and get it. Their action is purposeful and creates an impact. Others can experience this as arrogant or detached. Knowers are decisive and focused and do not welcome any form of distraction, whether it be unnecessary detail or unhelpful emotion.

So, a Thinker, a Feeler and a Knower go into a restaurant. The Thinker looks at the menu, processes the detail, probably uses some deductive reasoning to narrow down his choice and then, eventually, decides what he will order. The Feeler will mainly ignore the menu. She will look around the restaurant, look at what somebody else is eating, and see if she fancies it. She will have a word with the waiter and ask him what he recommends. Ultimately, she will go with mood, which is what she Feels. The Knower, on the other hand, will take a cursory glance at the menu and zone in quickly for the choices he would expect to make. He then orders decisively and without fuss. He then waits impatiently for the others to make their minds up.

How do you spot a Thinker shopping? She will usually have a list. Thinkers like plans and structures. They like to put their thoughts down in an orderly process. They like clarity and will execute their actions according to a thought-through process. The Feeler goes with the moment. He will be attracted by any energy source that tantalizes the senses, such as color, taste and smell. This shopper will be a victim of the fashion purchase and the spontaneous sale. In the supermarket he will be drawn to the color and vibrancy of the vegetable and fruit section. What about the Knowing shopper? Easy: no fuss. Just get the job done. Know what you want to get, get it, pay for it and get out.

What about our homes? What does a Thinker's house look like? And a Feeler's? And a Knower's? The Thinker's will be tidy and organized, with everything in its place. The CDs will be arranged in order and the cupboards will be neatly arranged. The Feeler's will be 'lived in', which could be anything from untidy to homely. There will be cushions and signs of spontaneity throughout. The Knower's home will be minimalist. The knower likes space. Everything should have a purpose and should work. The place should not be cluttered by meaningless or untidy distractions. It might be interesting to reflect on your own home: what is its style? Does it reflect your own style or that of your partner's? Or is it a combination of the two with different styles accommodated in distinct parts of the home?

The signs of our preferences are everywhere. It could be in the way that we eat our meals, the way we play sport, the way we encounter others. Why does this matter? Because understanding the preferences of those we are trying to communicate with can be critical to making the connection with them. The styles are like different languages. If we speak in 'Think' we use detail and tend to be precise and structured in our language. For the Thinker it has to make logical sense. The energy of Think is neutral, which means it is not animated or excitable, more work-like and matter-of-fact. Nothing wrong with this, but what if we are trying to communicate with a Feeler? Feelers like energy and the neutral tone of the Thinker will feel flat, even boring. Feelers are less directly interested in logic or detail. They want to be engaged, energized. Give them color, pictures and stories. So what chance of an easy connection between Thinker and Feeler?

And what about the Knower? He just wants you to get to the point. Give him the conclusion, and he will instantaneously take a position. It's either a yes or a no. There is no sitting on the fence. If he likes the first impression, he may then look for some evidence to back it up (if his secondary style is Think), or he may turn to a trusted friend or colleague (if his secondary style is Feel) to check it out with them.

So, if the Thinker throws detail at the Knower or the Feeler he or she will disconnect. If the Feeler goes off into storyland with the Knower, he will walk away. The Knower's style will typically frustrate the Thinker because he does not often explain the rationale behind his thinking or give the facts to back it up. It will frustrate the Feeler because the message is typically delivered without compassion or engagement. Here is the answer – take it or leave it.

At this point, I would encourage you to reflect on your own style and how it may affect the relationships in your life. Think about those you easily connect with and those you don't. All too often our ability, or inability, to connect with others will quickly determine whether we become friends or successful colleagues. This initial communication hurdle can be decisive, yet there is so much more to offer each other if we can be more flexible in our communication and our understanding. This principle applies whether we are discussing personal relationships in everyday life or if we are talking about global relationships between countries, cultures or religions. So this is a cause worth investing in.

My proposition is this: if we wish to improve our lives, and most of us do to one degree or another, it is best that we know from where we are starting. Our own experience of life is likely to tell us that people do not change their behavior easily. The more attached we are to our existing beliefs and habits, the more challenging personal change will be. Yet we equally understand that behaving as we have always done is likely to produce the same results as it always has.

And change is not just about what's happening on the outside. To have a realistic chance to change, we need to understand what is happening on the inside, that is, to understand how we 'tick' as human beings. Complete knowledge on such a vast subject is, of course, only as close as the horizon, but every step we take in the right direction will shed new light on our capabilities and will enrich our journey of discovery along the way.

So, can people really change? I don't mean the learning of new techniques that are useful but emotionless. I mean can we really change the way we Think, Feel and Know?

Before going further, it is necessary to return to further science. Our behavioral responses are not driven by the brain alone. We also need to consider the role of our heart and the autonomic nervous system and their effect on our behavior.

The role of the heart in behavior

"It is only with the heart that one can see rightly; what is essential is invisible to the eye."

—Antoine de Saint-Exupéry, French writer and aviator (1900-1944)

The heart and the autonomic nervous system

"What comes from the heart, goes to the heart."

—Samuel Taylor Coleridge (1772-1834)

I explained earlier the role of the amygdala and hippocampus in triggering our response to threat. I explained that this perception of threat is based on a combination of our genetic instincts and our life experiences. When the amygdala perceives a threat it activates the body's autonomic nervous system (ANS) and this in turn kicks off a chain reaction that gears the body to react in the desired way.

The ANS is the part of our nervous system that regulates many of the autonomic systems within our body, which means it does so without any need for conscious input from the cortex or Thinking brain. This would include the hormonal system, respiration, heart rate, blood pressure, hunger, thirst and temperature controls. Regulation is effected either through the sympathetic pathway, for instance when there is a need to speed up the systems, or through the parasympathetic pathway when the need is to slow down. The sympathetic system is effectively the 'fight or flight' response, whereas the parasympathetic system is 'rest or digest'.

Therefore, when the amygdala has signaled a threat, the ANS is activated, adrenalin is secreted from the adrenal glands and the heart becomes highly aroused as it prepares the body for immediate response. Adrenalin here acts as the priming agent, or petrol, of the body. Blood circulation is increased, and signals are sent through the motor-neural nervous system (which controls our muscles and movement) to generate the required physical response. All this happens in a split-second. We have all experienced this, the momentary response when we find our heart bursting and our senses primed. We will stay in this state until we believe that the threat has subsided. At this point, adrenalin production will reduce and another hormone, acetylcholine, will take its place in order to bring about a calming response. This is the body's way of 'warming down' and resuming normal operation. So, we can think of adrenalin as the accelerator of our body and acetylcholine as the brake. If used well together, they will take us through life navigating the scenarios we encounter with natural response and optimized energy.

So far, I have talked about response to threat. Yet, actually the same applies when we perceive an opportunity. Whereas threat is about the fear response, opportunity generates excitement and is generally perceived as a positive experience. Initially, the ANS response is the same in triggering adrenalin to prime the body for action. But it doesn't stay the same. We all know that our emotional experience of threat is very different from that of excitement. So while the first part of the priming process is the same, the next stage of the chain reaction is fundamentally different.

Here we have to understand the function of two further hormones: cortisol and dehydroepiandrosterone (DHEA).

Cortisol is often referred to as the body's 'stress hormone'. When the initial scenario that triggered the amygdala response is perceived as negative, that is, as a threat, the body primes itself for attack. Cortisol is a natural defence hormone whose function is to fight off the threat of trauma and infection. It is an anti-inflammatory and will be directed to those parts of the body perceived to be under attack. It therefore forms a critical part of our immune system response. People in sport will recognize the use of cortisone injections to ease the pain and swelling of injuries. Its role, therefore, is entirely protective.

DHEA, on the other hand, is triggered when the expectation is of a positive experience: this could range from the opportunity to make love with someone to whom you are highly attracted, to the chance to make a critical point in a public debate. DHEA is a key component in the production of oestrogen and testosterone and is fundamental in the body's reproductive system. It is a core part of the life-creation process. When released into the body, the effects are entirely positive, giving energy and a deep sense of achievement and satisfaction. Its full potential is yet to be discovered and, just as cortisone is available synthetically as a pain-killing agent, DHEA has also been made available in the treatment of fertility and even in attempts at anti-aging treatments.

So, to recap: the perception of threat or opportunity will trigger a high arousal response by releasing adrenalin into the body. If we perceive a negative response cortisol will be produced to protect us from attack. If the perception is positive, DHEA will be triggered, and we will feel we can conquer the world. Acetylcholine will resume normal operation when the initial trigger has subsided.

So, why then is this important in understanding human behavior? This is because the perception of threat or opportunity sits at the heart of our responses. The fear response, while there to protect us, can also hold us back when it comes to personal growth and behavior change. When we perceive threat, our instincts will direct us to stick with what we know, what we would more readily label our 'comfort area'. Anything outside this represents danger. If we cannot see opportunities through the barrier of fear, we are doomed to stay marooned on our defensive island. The fortress we build to protect us can easily become the prison that enslaves and isolates us.

To understand this in context, we need to remind ourselves that the physiology of our brain has been laid down over hundreds of thousands of years. Stone Age men and women faced huge physical survival challenges. Their brains evolved with a focus on threat and survival. The male of the species developed brains that focused on spatial awareness and targeted activity, such as hunting: theirs were the skills of judging pace, distance and movement, critical to the capturing of their prey and the avoidance of predators. The female nurtured her skills of protecting the family and watching for the immediate risks around the 'nest'. The threat of snakes and poisonous spiders abounded. Both were focused on the skills that would allow the family unit, and indeed the species, to survive. This legacy remains with us.

Of course, we are rarely faced with threats of physical survival in the west today, but we have created a society where social threat can be almost as damaging. Now that history and evolution has allowed us to raise our expectations of life, we are concerned with social value, peer opinions, maintaining status and grooming our egos. The threat of losing face in a public situation will kick off the same physiological response as the physical threat perceived by our ancestors.

Our brains are still far more tuned to looking for threat than opportunity. For example, the normal physiology of our modern bodies means that we typically see cortisol outweigh DHEA by a ratio of about 70:30, even for the less stressed among us. Evolution has allowed us to handle this. Unfortunately, many of us operate at a ratio of more like 90:10, which is when our internal systems start to break down, possibly leading to ill-health and potential fatality. There is a significant correlation between stress and cancer.

Therefore, any attempt to get people to take the 'risk' of behavior change will face the challenge of history and physiology stacking the odds against the willingness and ability to change. The more we perceive threat, the more we are geared to look for protection in what we already know. We seek solace in that which we have experienced before. Much research has been done to show that uncertainty is the greatest source of stress we face. When we have no internal reference point that can 'give us the answer', the alarm bells keep ringing all around our body. Even at times of greatest threat if we are given some sort of clarity we will see our stress levels reduce, as we now feel we have some level of control. The unknown is the greatest fear of all.

However, this does not mean that we cannot change. Part of the purpose of this book is to examine what can be done to support personal change using the principles and insight offered by the emerging science. Change is not easy, but it is possible.

The heart and the neurological system

"Always do right. This will gratify some people, and astonish the rest."

—Mark Twain (1835-1910)

Once considered little more than a sophisticated pump for circulating blood around the body, the evidence now emerging is of a supreme neurological unit, the role of which rivals and sometimes surpasses the brain in mastery of the physiological balance of the body. The main neurological connection between the heart and the brain is the vagus nerve (sometimes referred to as 'the pneumogastric nerve' or 'cranial nerve X'). This serves as the communication interface to enable effective collaboration between two of the body's most critical organs. The most recent research has shown that there are times when instructions sent to the heart by the brain are ignored: the heart momentarily becomes its own master. The brain and heart should not be considered master and slave, more partners playing to each other's strengths. Most of the heart's work is performed subconsciously, that is without conscious input from the cortex. For the most part, the heart operates according to its own operating instructions. We do not tell it what to do or how to do it.

Central to our understanding of the heart and its role as a neurological unit in the body is the energy it generates and distributes. It can be considered the power-house of the human body. It generates approximately 50 times the electrical output of the brain, supplying more than 2.5W of power. It generates an electro-magnetic signal that is at least 1,000 times greater than that of the brain. Its electrical signal is distributed to every cell in our body. In fact, this signal is transmitted outside of our body to a typical distance of approximately 5ft (1.5m).

The electrical output of the heart has become a critical measure in the monitoring of our cardiovascular health, typically by the use of the electrocardiogram (ECG). The level of output and variability of our heart rhythms is hugely informative in the diagnosis of health risks and treatments. Each heartbeat provides the trained specialist with a rich source of data. By tracking the level and frequency of the heart's electrical output (known as heart rate variability) we are able to gain vital insights into our physical health.

The electrical beat of the heart triggers energetic reactions throughout the body. It uses energy as a communication medium. The radiation of the heart's beat acts as a central point of synchronization for other neurological units in the body, rather like the conductor stepping up to set the pace and rhythm of the orchestra. Each musician has his or her music sheet to follow, instructions specific to the performance of the instrument concerned. Yet, without a conductor, the total effect of all the musicians performing to their own instructions is likely to be less than pleasing, and certainly not as good as it could be.

The body is a total organism, and it is the heart that physiologically regulates the performance of the whole – like the conductor who synchronizes the performance of the constituent parts. And the medium for this synchronization is energy. By producing a particular level of electrical output at a specific frequency, the heart calls the neurological units of the body into line to create the total effect. In this orchestra sits the brain itself, the heart and a number of 'mini-brains' (which is exactly the term used by a neurologist colleague). These mini-brains exist in the gut (the enteric brain), and in the neck where they control blood circulation and respiration. Without the heart's intervention they are largely independent units following their own path. Yet, when the heart steps up to conduct, the orchestra follows.

I will return to this subject again later in the book when we start to examine advanced performance. However, for now, let's continue to develop our understanding of just how significant and influential the heart is – not just physiologically but also in shaping our behavior.

When I was studying at university in the 1970s, I recall coming across research that showed that for many years, dentists as a profession have traditionally suffered with an unusually high mortality rate. While being a well-paid profession, their survival beyond retirement age was much less than other professions. At that time psychologists put this down to 'stress transfer'. By dealing with stressed patients on a daily basis it was considered inevitable that the dentists themselves would suffer accumulative stress. The theory was centered mainly on a psychological experience, which means that the mental experience of coping with this would itself, over a period of time, cause the dentist to become stressed. It all seems very logical and I am sure it still makes sense. However, current technology has shown us that something else is also happening.

The issue is also one of the physical proximity of the respective hearts of the dentist and patient. I have explained above that the heart radiates electro-magnetic energy outside the body. This translates into a form of direct communication going on between the respective hearts of the dentist and patient. Laboratory research has shown that the heart rhythms of the patient are directly transmitted to the heart of the dentist while in close proximity. It's like holding an active mobile phone to the radio; the result is audible interference – only in the case of the dentist there is no visible or audible sign and only appropriately placed electrical sensors can display the effects.

For me, this represents a great parallel for the affect of neurological data on traditional psychology. It is not that the psychologists of the last century were wrong or incompetent: far from it. It was more directly that they were not able to support their theories with data from live brains. Current research data, including functional MRI scans, has gone a long way to overcoming this limitation. Instead of developing theories based on statistical correlations of observed behavior patterns, we now have the opportunity to directly examine brain activity in relation to specific triggers, behaviors and experiences. We are moving from an observational model to an explanatory model.

So we now understand that our affect on one another in social situations is not just a psychological experience; it also takes place at the physical level. People who are seen to have gravitas are people who are centered in their own energy and who therefore project a strong electro-magnetic signal. Groups who influence one another do not do so just by mental transfer but also by energetic transfer. The phrase 'group think' is too limited, as it underplays the energetic dimension. So when groups get together and become excited it is like a mass adrenalin effect. There is a mass energetic and electro-magnetic transfer going on that has a multiplying effect. This has little to do with logic or the simple rational alignment of minds.

We see this on a regular basis at sports games. Any professional athlete will testify to the power of the crowd and how its energetic mood can directly affect the players. The notion of the home advantage in sports games is based on this principle. And, on a more sinister level, we have seen group energy take over when lynch mobs are activated. In this highly aroused environment rationality goes out of the window. It can only attempt to sort out the mess afterwards, but the damage has already been done.

The heart and memory

"Yesterday is history. Tomorrow is a mystery. And today? Today is a gift. That's why we call it the present."

—Babatunde Olatunji, Nigerian drummer, educator and social activist (1927-2003)

Let's take this a stage further and examine another area where we can see that our understanding of the role of the heart needs some rethinking, that of the heart and memory.

Early experiences of heart-transplant surgery demonstrated that the heart is capable of not only surviving for some time outside of a human body but is then also capable of successfully adapting its role in a new human host. This is a well-researched, tested and predictable outcome of advanced surgery. However, heart-transplant surgery and the ensuing results for the recipient patient have also thrown up a much more surprising insight.

In clinical medical terms, heart-transplant surgery is a well-established mainstream activity, yet the after effects for the living recipient are still producing new data. There are a number of well-publicized cases where the new heart has not only affected the recipient physiologically (which was the original purpose of the surgery) but also appears to have done so in behavior. A particular case involved a man receiving a heart from a donor who was a classical musician. The normal approach is to largely preserve the anonymity of the donor to the recipient. After the physiological benefits of the surgery had kicked-in and the transplant was considered a success, the recipient found himself strangely drawn to classical music, despite having no interest whatsoever in this before the surgery. The attraction became so great that he felt compelled to learn to play the violin. Despite no previous experience of playing classical music, his progress in acquiring the skill to play the violin was astounding. How could this be?

This is only one of many cases with similar experiences. So, it seems that when we transplant the heart of someone to somebody else, we transplant some of the donor's personality. Let's try to explain this.

First, I should clarify what I mean by 'personality'. For me this means the totality of the persona we present to the outside world. 'Personality' is usually a term attributed by others to us and represents what they experience in interacting with us. Terms like 'enthusiastic', 'serious', 'spiritual' and 'boring' come to mind. It cannot truly represent the total dynamic of how we experience our own existence, but it is a very loose summary of the way we present ourselves to others.

The case above covers the acquisition of a new interest and a skill to a very high standard that was difficult to understand without taking into account the experience and skill-set of the donor. In the same way, other heart recipients have been recorded as experiencing very different emotions following surgery, feelings that they would not normally associate with themselves.

The answer, it appears, lies in understanding memory. My understanding here is less based on available research but more on the private access I have had to the neurological profession. There is no way I can do justice to an explanation of the complex process of memory, but the fundamental principles are intriguing. The current understanding is that memory is not limited to storage in the brain. Yes, there are memory centers in the brain that contribute significantly to our ability to store memory and to access it but there also appears to be a role played by the heart and even across the cellular structure of our bodies. It seems that the brain and heart work together in sharing memory. Neurologists themselves do not have the total explanation and are not in complete agreement as to how exactly this works: hardly surprising in an area of emerging science. Yet it does start to throw some light on how heart transplants may also affect personality and behavior.

Our memory is, after all, the foundation of our behavior. Not only do we memorize the motor-neural techniques involved in executing specific tasks, such as those mastered by the violinist, but we constantly refer to our memory of life experiences in order to react to the choices available to us today. We cannot help this. Our memories are by their very nature emotional experiences captured visually and associatively.

Consider for a moment the power of this through something as simple as music. Randomly, a song comes on the radio that we have not heard for many years. Despite having been outside of our conscious reach, the song now immediately evokes the memory of where and when we heard it previously and exactly how we felt at the time – a visual and emotional testimony to a recalled experience. Not only can we remember the experience, but we also find ourselves remembering the lyrics. This is associative recall. The neurological system has conjured up the relevant connections in memory to give us the best possible recall of the event. The more emotionally powerful the memory, the stronger the recall. This is of course why trauma is so difficult to eradicate from our memories; it is laid down in the deepest recesses of our mind. Memory sits at the heart of our behavior, and our hearts sit at the core of our memory.

By now, I hope you are getting the picture that our hearts play a very significant role in affecting our energy and the behavioral reactions that result from this. This is no romantic myth or artistic concept; it is demonstrable by science. The saying 'hearts and minds' rings scientifically truer today than ever.

Section III:

Everyday reality

*"It is not in the pursuit of happiness that we find fulfilment,
it is in the happiness of pursuit."*

**—Denis Waitley, American motivational speaker
and writer (1933-)**

One-to-one

I now want to translate the scientific principles of section II into examples of everyday reality. I trust this will offer you value, whether you are involved directly in the field of influencing human behavior, such as a businessperson, leader, manager, coach, consultant, counselor or trainer, or whether you are just interested in what makes people tick. To do this I will draw on my experience in business, as the CEO of a corporate business and as a coach. In particular I will interpret and relate some of the experiences of my clients and colleagues. I will also refer to experiences that I have encountered in areas such as sport and prisons. I will look at this subject matter at four levels: the individual, relationships, teams, and organizations.

Ourselves

"Always be a first-rate version of yourself, instead of a second-rate version of somebody else."

—Judy Garland (born Frances Ethel Gumm) (1922-1969)

This is, of course, the best place to start. Understanding ourselves is central to any chance of personal change, and most of us believe that we could handle certain things in our lives better. Furthermore, if we can understand the opportunities for change in ourselves, as well as the barriers, it gives us great insight into how we may support others to bring about change in their lives. Why ignore the most available source of data – ourselves?

So let's reflect on life's journey for each of us. We were genetically created by our biological parents and brought into this world by our mother. Even in the womb we start to collect data about how we experience life. We have been created with a set of genetic programmes called instincts, and they will give us a reasonable chance of survival. Inevitably, these genetic programmes lack personalized data, as we have not lived before. So we populate the programmes with data from our experiences.

At this early stage in our life, there is minimal cognitive capability: it is all about instincts and sensations. The baby crying at birth is still operating instinctively, as she follows her genetic program for attracting attention and support from her mother. And those of us who have been on the receiving end of a baby's crying know that the noise a baby makes is honed to perfection and virtually impossible to ignore. It strikes us where it hurts most, directly in the heart. Whether the baby is experiencing the emotion of actually feeling upset at this time is debatable, although this will evolve quite quickly. The baby will learn by repeating its experiences and will come to understand the link between crying and getting attention. It will then build an expectation of this response from her mother. If this response is not repeated the survival instinct will kick in again and further energetic responses will be generated.

Therefore, our early experiences are the basis of the data foundation for our memory. This is so powerful because there is no other data. Life is writing on an empty page. There is no data clogging, no unlearning required. Children are copying machines. Their instincts guide them to copy the behavior of those around them. Initially, they know nothing else. Then they will build a memory of the consequences of their copying. If the result was positive, for example, getting fed or receiving acknowledgment from her parents, the baby will be inclined to repeat the behavior. If the result was negative, for example, getting hurt or told off, she is less likely to repeat the pattern of behavior. This is why positive reinforcement in young children is so powerful. Of course, they also need to understand what constitutes unacceptable behavior, but there is an important balance to be achieved between instructing the child and frightening her. Fear responses can help us to survive in dangerous situations but they close down our openness to learning as the body simply responds to feeling under threat and 'pulls up the drawbridge'.

As our childhood progresses, so does our cortex develop. This dramatically accelerates our ability to reason, reflect, learn and generally make sense of our surroundings. While the parents have the primary responsibility for nurturing the early emotional character of the child, the development of the cortex needs the support of our schooling system. Traditionally, the main focus of western education systems has been the development of intellect, although this will vary across countries and cultures. And it is not only the education that is provided by the teacher. There is as much to be learned in the schoolyard regarding the development of relationships with our school mates. Mom and Dad may have given us the rules for social engagement, but they cannot apply them for us. So, day-by-day, we build our learning and capability to interact with others, the constant laying down of experiences in our memory as a reference base for our own life's journey.

Then comes adolescence. From the age of puberty to the late teens and early 20s, our bodies go through huge changes triggered by hormonal developments in our body chemistry. Not only do we have to contend with our physical shapes altering before our very eyes, but the reality of our emerging sexuality: simultaneously exciting, scary and confusing. And remember, at this age we do not have sufficient life experience captured in memory to help us navigate our way through an entirely new experience.

Therefore, the teenager looks to others for her answers. In the early days she could rely on Mom and Dad, but when she went to school she found that the teacher gave some different answers. Then there are the friends and peers who throw in another set of opinions to make life even more confusing. So the teenager either collapses under the pressure of this gathering fog or she fights back and takes control. Adolescence is a very energetic period when we are inclined towards experimentation, overreaction, mood swings, withdrawal and excitement. The same inner forces that drive this energy will convince the teenager that she should take a grip of life's answers for herself. Clearly nobody else can be totally relied on for all the answers, so it is time to make up her own. Yet, as I have said, she lacks the depth of life experience to work out what those answers are. But at this age, who cares? 'Talk to the hand, the face isn't listening; I have the answers anyway.'

Here comes the initial formulation of the ego.

By 'ego' here, I am not specifically referring to Freud's original definition, although it is along the same lines. Equally, I am not presenting ego here as a bad thing. The term is often used in modern parlance to identify those with high opinions of themselves – he has a 'big ego'. I have no such judgment here. For me, the ego is the position in society we set out to create for ourselves; it is our 'outer self'. It typically starts at this time of life, when we feel the need to decide who we are and how we want to present ourselves to the world.

I remember in my teens that I was impressed by strong silent males, so I chose to embark upon this route, probably as a suitable route for attracting females. Likewise, I made the commitment to build a successful career and going to university was inevitably a part of my plan. In parallel, I loved sport and socializing and I would never have any hang-ups about enjoying myself. This was the theme that was emerging, a sort of work hard–play hard philosophy, with plenty of room for the opposite sex. No rocket science here then – just understandable steps in the initial creation of my position in the world and a series of incremental decisions that reflected the influences of those who most mattered to me: my family, friends and advisers.

Of course, there is catch-22 here. If we don't take a position or create the ego that we present to the world, we have no platform for personal growth. We become emotionally intelligent by learning from the experiences we appear to create in others as well as those we create in ourselves. If we are not putting an ego position out there we will get no response. We cannot live our lives just blowing in the wind if we are to give ourselves some sense of direction. So we have to do it. Yet we are doing it at a time in our lives when we are emotionally immature and limited in life experience. In the language of this book, we seek the certainty of a Knowing position but we do so without sufficient depth of experience to anchor our position in a place of integrity and confidence. It is often a false-Knowing, without depth – hence the tendency of the teenager to get excitable or to withdraw when he feels that his position is being challenged. He is trying to deal with his own uncertainties and having those closest to him present him with more challenges is not always the most productive route forward, as many parents will testify.

You may recall that earlier in the book I referred to the pre-frontal cortex as the part of the brain charged with making sense of the self. Research has shown that this process is normally complete by the age of 24. As a parent, I am tempted to say that you should wait until then before you can expect to get any sense out of your offspring. But I dare not say that – my kids would kill me. Actually it does seem to make sense. By then, the heavy hormonally driven behavior of the adolescent has largely stabilized. We have typically left the education system and are accumulating real life experience of having to support ourselves. We feel for the first time that a picture of ourselves is emerging.

God bless the ego. We have created it to protect us on life's journey, to present a consistent image to the world and also to save for ourselves the bits of us we do not want to expose because they are still a work-in-progress. However, once we have created the ego, we have to continue to feed it. It is not real. It is our own personal creation. It can only survive if we continue to reaffirm it. None of this is a problem if we have got our initial position right. Yet at this stage of life we still have so much to learn about ourselves that the chances of getting it right are extremely remote. Therefore, while created to protect us and to give us a base from which to experience life, the ego can become a trap that distracts us from who we really are. Life moves on, expectations change, our own needs evolve, different relationships move into and out of our lives, but the ego will seek to hold on to its position as the only reason for its existence. And when that position no longer serves us it will fight like hell to survive. Letting go of our ego is one of the biggest challenges in personal change. It has been our comfort blanket in life and, when the time comes to remove it, it can feel cold and scary.

And, of course, life is a journey with many periods of growth and plateau. Within my coaching business we talk about the 'brick walls' that all people face at critical times in their lives. As we go through each leg of our journey, we will inevitably face the 'first brick wall', which is when we have to make our minds up about what this part of the journey is really about. If we get focused and clear about what we want to achieve we will pass through the wall, and our energetic investment will start to pay off as we experience personal growth. This growth can be both personal and commercial. The same principles apply whether we are talking about personal journeys, relationship journeys or business journeys.

As we move through this growth period, we can enjoy the benefits of success. Yet the basis for our success will change. People move on, their expectations change, their challenges change: relationships evolve and businesses and markets move on. Gradually a feeling of growth will turn into a feeling of frustration and eventually stress. This is the 'second brick wall'. Unlike the first, we have now experienced success, but we can feel it slipping away. Therefore, whereas the first wall was about making your mind up and focusing your energy, the second is all about reinvention. Our proposition for success is no longer working as well as we would choose. For the 'successful' executive this could mean that her career star is no longer shining so brightly. She is starting to reach her career plateau. Alternatively, the outward signs may be OK, but inwardly she feels she is paying too high a personal price for her career. In relationships, the dynamic has changed and become boring or confrontational. In business, the top team may have lost its way: it knew how to succeed in the past, but it is not clear about how to do so in the future. The principles are the same.

I spend a lot of my time coaching senior business executives at a one-to-one level, normally a CEO, Vice President or Director and typically in large corporate businesses. Many of these clients are facing second brick wall issues, and we aim to work through how they wish to react. First and foremost, no coaching can work without building trust. The currency of the coaching engagement is energy. Without arousing an energetic response in your client, there is no prospect of personal change. This does not mean getting excited or emotional: it means recognizing that mobilization to action comes in Feeling. You and your client will have to connect at a relationship level if there is to be progress.

Once some form of trusting relationship is in place, the usual challenge is helping the client to understand that reinvention here means *personal* reinvention. The predictable early dialog is about how everything else has to change: the organization structure, the reporting rules, the boss, colleagues and customers. The client needs to be guided very carefully to look in the mirror. Judging his energy and getting the timing right for the right questions are all central to making progress.

I was confronted recently by a typical challenge from a CEO to whom I had been recommended by a colleague. In obvious Knowing style he went straight for the jugular even before I had sat down, looking straight into my eyes and asking very abruptly: 'So, what value do you bring?' This was, of course, a defining moment when we would either connect or disconnect: and if you don't get off to a good start with a Knower it is usually very difficult to recover. There was no time to analyze or work out where he was coming from, so I just gave him my honest, instinctive answer. I smiled and said, 'I help CEOs to stay sane.' He smiled back, and we got on with what turned out to be a very productive conversation.

When I reflected on this experience, there were some interesting observations. The obvious one is that this was not an answer I had ever given before to any similar question; yet somehow it felt right. Second, my experience of coaching and my enjoyment of it, as well as my experience of Knowers (and I knew instantly that he was a primary Knower) meant that I saw no threat in the moment. This enabled me to stay calm and to even enjoy the encounter. Instinctively I knew my intentions were good and my integrity was not in question. This was just a guy using the style he understood best.

My point here is not to write the next coaching manual; there are plenty of those already available. Equally, I have no desire to create the next management theory. I have been saturated with them throughout my career, and I have found that most of them do not work. My clients have said to me on a number of occasions that the last thing they need is another management theory. What they really want is help with the application. What I aim to do here is offer you real-life snapshots of my client experiences to demonstrate directly how the principles already explained in this book do indeed directly affect our behavior and experience of life. The value comes at the point of application.

Client snapshots

"The most basic of all human needs is the need to understand and be understood.
The best way to understand people is to listen to them."

—Ralph Nichols, English badminton player (1910-2001)

So let's have a look at some real-life and business examples. Interspersed over the next few sections are snapshots of real client experiences that I believe will help you to add depth to your understanding of the Think Feel Know model.

Let's start with three examples here of primary Think, primary Feel and primary Know. The cases shown later will be less clearcut.

Beth – the ultimate Thinker

Beth's primary style was Think, with a secondary Know. She was the managing partner of a mid-size business of high-caliber professional services people. Her intellectual prowess and driven behavior had taken her to the top of her profession, and she was held in very high esteem for her particular specialism. She and her partners had grown the business very successfully and were now looking to push down the accelerator further. There were two main focal points for our coaching dialog. The first was that she felt personally unhappy with the situation she found herself in; the second was that the relationships among the partners in the organization were not evolving in a way that best supported their business ambition.

Beth's source of personal unhappiness in her job was a complex matter, but a key element was that she had inadvertently created a state of dependence around her at the top team level. This was not done by design. In fact, Beth was a natural delegator when it involved more junior staff, and they would generally have seen her as an inspirational leader. But when it came to her peers she found it very difficult to have direct and honest work relationship discussions. These partners were close personal friends with great loyalty to each other. Beth was very aware of this and valued it highly; maybe too highly. There appeared to have been boundaries drawn between social activity and work activity, but there appeared to be no point of crossover: relationships in work were not discussed.

As the business grew and the level of expectation increased with it, occasionally partners would find themselves struggling either individually or as a team.

There was nothing exceptional in this, just the normal challenges of managing a growing business and the size and complexity of the task becoming more and more demanding. However, instead of creating an environment where they could openly discuss their mutual concerns within the team, Beth relied on her thinking prowess to engineer the discussions. This behavior came from a caring place. She was concerned that if the dialog about mutual performance became too open the result would be team upset and disharmony and, frankly, this was not something she could have handled easily.

Thus, confronted with this fear, the Thinking brain created a set of rules for engineering the discussions so that the risk of fall-out could be contained. Agendas were carefully planned and debate pre-positioned to avoid risk, and if they showed sign of drifting into dangerous water, Beth would pull them back and was always clever enough to back her actions with a solid intellectual argument. The loyalty of the team was such that they were in tacit agreement with this. They did not want to rock the boat. So they ended up with a mutually constraining pact that smothered the development of their working relationships. Not only was Beth frustrated but so were the team. While they were in willing deference to her style, they were also left with feelings of important matters left unsaid and unaddressed. And Beth herself was still carrying the burden of engineering the dialog, a heavy load that could only get heavier.

For me, this was a case of mis-match between the nature of the problem and the nature of the solution. Beth had applied a Think solution to a Feel problem. The problem was relationships, and relationships are all about energetic connection or disconnection. Relationship challenges by their very nature are emotional. There is no getting away from this. But Beth did not have the answer or the emotional experience of successfully managing relationship challenges. So she could not rely on her intuition here as there was no solution registered in the Knowing brain. She had not constructed a set of rules for dealing with such issues. So, she had to rely on what she did know, which was creating a structural and orderly approach to managing the dialog, rather like that of a courtroom.

For Beth to move forward on this, she had to let go of her Think dependency. Yes, there are sensible rules that can be applied to support and facilitate relationship discussions, but the reality is that people have to be able to express their energy. The alternative, which is suppression of emotions, is not sustainable. Emotional exchanges need to be facilitated in a safe environment. And Beth faced the challenge of not having the confidence in her own skill-set to be able to handle the emotional challenge. Ultimately, it was her own fear of being able to handle the feelings exchange that was inhibiting her, although she was rationalizing this as being worried for the team. Her challenge was to find the courage to let the team look after themselves and, even more importantly, to trust herself. She needed to give up her self-imposed sense of personal responsibility for the dialog; the partners would have to accept this responsibility for themselves, and, ironically, they were in most part willing to do so.

Freddie – holding back the emotions

Freddie had been in his organization for a long time. He had seen many changes and had given 100% commitment every step of the way. He was a very energetic personality. I was struck the first time I met him by the speed of his conversation. He articulated his thoughts very quickly to the extent that it was tiring keeping up with him. I was his coach, so it was my job to listen to him very carefully, but I wondered how others would cope if he were always this animated. Yet, he was a lovely guy, quick to smile and ready to engage. Have you worked out his profile yet? It was Feel/Think, that is primary Feel followed by secondary Think.

Freddie was a very emotional human. Like most corporate males, he did not always show it, which is why he typically tried to process rationally as fast as he could so that his thoughts could keep up with his feelings. In his case, the limbic layer was clearly in charge. He would respond emotionally to his situation and would then rely on his moderating cortex to keep his behavior in check. The style was therefore one of internalized emotion. In the company of friends and trusted colleagues he would openly wear his heart on his sleeve. If he was in a situation where he felt unable to be open, it meant he had to simply sit on his emotions. This would not always succeed and sometimes, although not very often, the frustration could boil over.

The reason I particularly want to use this example is because it is so common in corporate business. Yes, Freddie was exceptionally animated in his behavior, but there are many other examples of others who are constantly fighting their own internal battle of bottled-up feelings. My own experience suggests that males have more to bottle up anyway because we are conditioned this way. Add to this the unforgiving nature of corporate business and its response to those who step out of line and we have the absolute recipe for unexpressed feelings. Eventually this can only have one result for the individual, which is stress, and stress ultimately will result in damage to health. But the consequences here are negative not only for the individual but also for the organization. The repression of feelings has significant consequences for organizational culture, a subject I will return to later.

Fortunately, Freddie was very fit for his age and looked after himself very well. He had mastered the 'limitations' of his style (and we all have limitations) so that he could genuinely boast a long and successful career. Yet, when it came to the crunch he was very dependent on two things: first, the feeling that he could trust those that he worked for and with (Feel); second, a sense of purpose (Know). It was not that he did no Knowing: in fact, he had a very strong set of values that could not be easily overruled. However Freddie had performed service roles through most of his career. In service or support roles, the primary task is to serve the purpose of the client or the boss. He was therefore both conditioned to and comfortable with referencing out to his boss or client for business purpose. He was not only ready to connect with a purposeful boss, he needed that connection in order to channel his energy. Yet this sense of purpose had to stand the test of his own values. If they did, he would fight in the trenches for the cause; if they didn't, he would always struggle to connect.

In the earlier years of his career, Freddie had been blessed with people he could trust and a purpose he could believe in. When it got to the time that he felt he could not rely on either of these, it was time for him to leave the organization, and he did.

Charlie – harnessing the tiger

Charlie was a larger-than-life character whose career success had been built on passion, personal gravitas and a depth of knowledge of his particular industry sector. He was now president of a business division within a global business. In recent years the overall business had operated with largely independent operating businesses. They had grown rapidly in a technologically driven business sector. The overall organization was seen by many as a holding company, rather than as a day-to-day business operation. Consequently, different sub-cultures existed within the business with strong local loyalties. So, when the business decided that strategically it needed to operate more cohesively as a whole (not an unusual decision for a maturing business) it was about to take on major leadership and cultural alignment challenges.

This was very real for Charlie at a personal level. His very Knowing style meant that he thrived with space to operate his own way. He was not a natural team-worker. He was excellent at leading teams and creating loyalty in those closest to him, but, for him, you were in his team or you were not important. In the wider business he was either loved or disliked. His strength of personality made him a fearsome figure, someone you would prefer to have on your side rather than playing against you. His secondary style was Feeling. This was critical to his ability to take people with him. He was full of energy, and his enthusiasm washed over others. He now did very little Think; it was not that he was no longer able to process facts, figures and logic but more that he now constantly used his own intuition to guide him. For a man who had developed such a deep knowledge of his industry sector this made absolute sense.

Now, however, he was facing an organizational change that would place major demands on his personal style. The new organization would be a more complex operating unit with matrix management sitting at the heart. Those of us who have experienced matrix management (and that means most of us who have had management careers in the corporate business world) know that it presents difficult relationship challenges. For me, it is a rational structure for devolving power, but it rarely works well at the relationship level.

For Charlie it meant that collaboration with his colleagues was now becoming as important as his instincts. But collaboration works on the premise that all involved have a roughly equal contribution to make. In Charlie's mind, and more importantly in his heart, this was not the case. Nobody knew more about his sector than himself, a claim that few in the wider business would dispute. Yet leaving Charlie to totally run his show also presented concerns for the wider organization. Would he really work towards synergistic solutions with other business divisions? Would he support the development of a common vision across the business? Would he be able to adapt his style to represent something more appropriate to the corporate whole?

For me, the honest answer to all of these questions was – with difficulty. Charlie was not about to go down the road of 'compromise and bureaucracy' willingly. His whole life experience had taught him otherwise. Yet, now he was being asked to do this for the greater good. His superiors had presented him with good analytical and structural reasons as to why the changes made sense, but Charlie was a startling example of what we all really are: that ultimately we are driven by our emotions. By embarking on what felt to him like a more Think business environment, with its emphasis on control, data and systems, he was feeling frustrated and isolated from his peers. The main thrust of the organization's business dialog with him was about structure and compliance. Charlie needed freedom to operate and people he could trust.

Don't misunderstand me; his bosses had every right to pursue the path they were taking. The Think element of any business is critical if it is to avoid running blind or acting as a 'headless chicken'. On the other hand, a strategy dominated by Think misses the opportunity to connect with people. The culture becomes one of compliance rather than commitment. Charlie could recognize the rationale of the changes, but it gave him huge emotional and behavioral challenges. What they initially failed to do was openly acknowledge the nature of this challenge and work through how it could be resolved to mutual satisfaction. Fortunately, the organization had the insight to recommend coaching support to Charlie, and this has formed the basis of our ongoing one-to-one conversations.

As you read the rest of the snapshots I hope you will be able to see that the Think, Feel and Know styles can manifest themselves in very different blends and with a variety of results. This is a reflection of our own neurological makeup, and our current functioning reflects the constant interaction between the cortex, limbic and basal regions of the brain. The behavior that shows up is a reflection of which particular region is playing the primary behavioral role at the time. It would be a big mistake to use profiling to pigeonhole people, as, regrettably, many personality profiling tools are inclined to do. We can move between these states very rapidly. The key to a successful connection with a person is not to pigeonhole him as a particular type but more to understand the state he is in when you are trying to communicate with him. Knowing which part of his brain is influencing him most at the time is an important insight into how you can effectively engage with him. It is then a case of matching your style with his. This will be developed in the next chapter, which looks more specifically at relationships.

Relationships

"No one can make you feel inferior without your consent."

—(Anna) Eleanor Roosevelt,
First Lady of the United States (1884-1962)

Here I will briefly discuss relationships between two people. I will use the Think, Feel, Know model to simplify the interactive dynamics and hopefully to give you something you can start to use for yourselves in thinking about the key relationships in your life.

When I work with clients, especially client teams, I start by coaching them to profile key relationships in their lives outside of work. This is because I do not want them to see themselves simply as 'work-beings'. When working with the Think Feel Know model it is important to reflect on your whole self, not just that part of you that turns up for work. The next stage is to ask my clients to profile their team colleagues and to do so in a way that explains how they experience one another. Nobody can profile anyone other than through the way they process their own perceptual data. In this way, the acceptance of the profiler's own role in the perception is acknowledged. Critically, all judgment needs to be suspended. This is simply a conversation about styles, and there can be no room for what is good and what is bad if there is to be a constructive and open discussion.

When we do this profiling all three styles are taken into account for each individual because, as I have said, it is the blending and interplay of these styles that gives us our own. The Think Feel Know business offers an online indicator that allows people to get feedback on their styles split into percentiles. This can be helpful in illustrating how secondary styles come into play to create successful or unsuccessful pairing relationships. However, I feel that to explain the permutations of all the pairing profiles using all three styles would be labored, as this would involve covering 21 permutations in total: so here I will stick to the headliners, the primary styles that show up most for us in our lives, and we will examine the typical interaction between them. We can look at what is likely to work well for the relationship and what may present challenges. We will also look at why the different styles fall in love.

Using the Think/Feel/Know model and the primary styles there are six primary pairing profiles:

Think: Feel

Think: Know

Feel: Know

Think: Think

Feel: Feel

Know: Know

Client snapshot

Eve – keeping it real

Eve was a sophisticated, high-level operator in a global business. She had been with the business at its inception and had seen it grow to a billion dollar organization. Over her career she had honed her instincts and was very perceptive, particularly when it came to people-judgment. She was not tolerant of 'waffle' and liked people to get to the point, in true Knowing fashion. Her whole style was underpinned by a strong sense of Feel. She was not exuberant or demonstrative but was more of an understated Feeler who valued her close relationships very highly. She was not slow to take a position and thrived best when she was able to make an intuitive connection with her peers, one where they just 'got' one another and dialog did not need messy elaboration or validation. For Eve, the challenge was keeping her sense of purpose alive.

Knowers have to have a very clear sense of purpose, and there was nothing lacking here when the business started up. She helped to create highly energized and fiercely loyal relationships at the top level of the business. There was a shared sense of common purpose and direction. This was a critical factor in what became a very successful business. Her reputation was respected well beyond her discipline, and this is still the case today. However, along the way, relationships had evolved, the organization had become more structurally complex, and there was a self-evident need for a more systems-based approach to supporting the business. Eve was more than capable of guiding this, but it wasn't where her heart was. For her the business purpose had become less clear and there wasn't the same level of intuitive connection across the top team.

Thus the coaching conversation was all about reviving her sense of purpose, even if that meant leaving the organization she still loved. This took time. It started with getting in touch with the feelings that underpinned the frustration she was then feeling. Then came the articulation of these feelings. This does not have to be a fluffy session on the therapeutic couch: Eve's Knowing style would never have allowed that. But it did mean being honest about what was going on inside. Identifying key emotional drivers can be enough for Knowers, and sure enough she rebounded slowly but surely. This was then coupled with changes in her business that at least clarified some of the uncertainty. An opportunity was now being created for previous relationships to reconnect and new relationships to be formed. She started to feel valued again. It was not that her colleagues had behaved in a way that left her feeling unvalued: this was more her own emotional processing. Knowers need to be very clear about their 'core value proposition'. They need to know why they are there. This feeling cannot be faked. They are not the 'type' who can compromise for something they don't believe in. And as the organization faced up to its next chapter of growth, Eve could feel her sense of purpose reviving. She was back on board.

I will offer some insights into each of these pairings over the next few pages. However, this can only be simplistic. As I have shown earlier, the blend of each of the styles is different for each of us and manifests itself in varying behaviors.

Think: Feel

Typically, the Thinker in the relationship will seek out a rationale. He will want to understand things logically and be able to order his thoughts and activities in such a way that is well structured and reliable. Diligence is appreciated. His energy is typically neutral. This does not have to mean flat: it means matter-of-fact and workman-like. Thinkers like projects, and every project needs a project plan. After all, what is a plan other than a set of thought-through actions normally presented in a logical sequence? The Feeler, on the other hand, responds to energy. This energy can be expressed in the form of excitement and adventure, or it can be more passive, as in empathy and warmth. Following the trail of energy does not need detail; it means going with the flow and experiencing the journey in the moment. The energetic limbic region of the brain does not forecast the future; it leaves that to the cortex. She needs to be energized. If she doesn't get this she will become distracted or even volatile. Life with the unbridled Feeler may be exciting or hazardous, but it is never boring.

So the opportunities for disconnection are clear: the deliberate pace of Think v the spontaneity of Feel; the need for being organized in Think v the need not to feel boxed-in for Feel; the need for clarity and objectivity in Think v the need for 'impressionism' and subjectivity in Feel; and so on. Note the likely behavior of each member of the pair when the relationship is under pressure: when we feel most at risk, such as in arguments, we typically retreat to our primary style. In this case, in the heat of argument, the Thinker will look for rationality and logic as his savior. Precise language for him will be the only way forward. For the Feeler precision is largely irrelevant; it's all about subjective expression. Volatility will manifest itself in erratic behavior and colorful language. 'Swearing' itself is simply an energetic self-expression. It means nothing logically, but it can be a vital outlet for those in high Feel.

So, my advice to the Thinker in an argument with a Feeler is *don't overanalyze*. Deal with the energy by creating an emotional (not a logical) bridge that can allow the Feeler to feel less threatened. This can be, for instance, a hug or a calming (not a patronizing) voice. In the moment, she needs to feel acknowledged. Only then can thinking be allowed to play its part. The brain will need to feel less threatened before it can collaborate with the heart to return the oxygenated blood supply to those parts of the cortex that can offer objectivity and perspective. This will not happen immediately.

And my advice to the Feeler in an argument? Simply put, it is *calm down*. We all know that saying this to someone in high Feel is not usually productive, but it is the only way forward. In that moment the challenge is the Feeler herself not any third party. The perception of immediate threat has to be addressed and removed by reference to one of two main options. The first of these is reference to a more powerful memory, purpose or vision. Referring to something that matters more can be a powerful stabilizer. In relationships this could be a simple reminder that, while you are arguing about your child having been out too late, she is now home safe. The second option is to move into Think. This means trying to return to a more logical analysis of the situation. A practical suggestion is writing things down. The content of the writing may make more or less sense, but the simple act of engaging the cortex in the writing should bring with it a more neutral energy that may help to calm the situation.

If this fails because the level of energetic arousal has gone too far off the scale you may be able to calm yourself by focusing on your breathing (explained further in section IV). If all else fails remove yourself from the scene and return to the interchange when you have had time to process your feelings, and you are able to engage in more measured dialog.

Note: I am not taking sides here; I am simply dealing with the dynamics of the interaction and the behavioral choices available to each party. So how on earth would these relationships ever work? In everyday life, the Thinker and Feeler described above can ameliorate their differences by moving to the styles where they can both connect. This may be the secondary style for the Thinker, who can easily move into Feel, or vice versa. This is where the understanding of all three styles would come into play.

However, there is a more powerful and fundamental explanation. None of us can exist or feel entirely complete on our own. We develop our picture of ourselves through life as we create an effect on others, and we get feedback about that impact. The feedback may not always be sought, but it is always available in the reactions of others. Even so-called hermits typically have relationships with animals. A solitary monk gives himself up to meditation in order to develop his relationship with his spiritual source. To live life completely without somebody to respond to us means we will lose any sense of identity of who we are. It would be a form of sensory deprivation that would likely result in insanity.

So the Thinker falls in love with the Feeler because she gives him permission to 'let go', to have fun, to bring some excitement and spontaneity into his life. Thinkers can be bound by their own rules of social engagement. Having a relationship with someone who can show you very easily how to set aside these self-imposed limitations can be highly rewarding. On the other hand, for the Feeler, experiencing on her own a life of emotional ups and downs can be scary, with no one to moderate the extremes. Thinkers bring stability and organization to a world that could otherwise feel chaotic. Their sense of perspective and ability to think things through can offer a sometimes sorely needed source of practical guidance. Our styles do not have to be the same for our relationship to succeed; it is what we do to make the most of our styles that will decide whether the relationship succeeds or fails.

Think: Know

The picture of the Thinker has been painted in the last example. So, let's remind ourselves about the Knower. Knowing behavior is uncompromising. A Knower expects to get his own way, or he will withdraw. He will bring a sense of purpose to the relationship if he is allowed, and he will do so without any fuss. In his mind he, quite simply, is right. He will take a position very quickly and will not expect to be challenged. He will expect to be the decision-maker on the things that matter to him, and he will deem the things that do not matter to him to be irrelevant. Thus, in a relationship he will expect to have his own space respected. Knowing is fiercely independent and, of itself, does not need a relationship. The relationship need primarily comes from Feel.

Why then would Thinkers be attracted to Knowers and vice versa? A Thinker sees a Knower as a source of direction and purpose. A Knower is very decisive about what is right and what is wrong and can therefore provide the Thinker with clarity. Thinking in and of itself can become mundane and can lack meaning if it is overplayed over time. While the Thinker is drawn to the detail, the Knower will look to the bigger picture. This is where the relationship is at its most compatible, as the Knower avoids the detail. He likes to charge off in his own direction, even if that means leaving a trail of mess behind him. The Thinker hoovers up the mess and does so willingly because this is what she is good at. Knowing can be single-minded and high risk – "My way or the highway." Yet, he will not be able to stay in Knowing permanently, and when he emerges from his self-imposed exile, he will find comfort in the reliability and thoroughness of the Thinker. Knowing can be isolating in its effect and returning to the stability and realism of the Thinker can be a place of solace and grounding.

I feel the need to balance this picture as, so far, there appears to be no Feel in this relationship. In reality, a relationship without Feel has no warmth or affection. It is simply an arrangement or a transactional partnership. Successful relationships between primary Thinkers and primary Knowers will have to connect in Feel as either the second or third style preferences. It does not mean that they do not care for each other: they may do so very deeply. It is more that they are less inclined to demonstrate Feeling behavior in expressing their emotions.

So what happens when these two fall out? While the Thinker will seek logic, data and rules of engagement, the Knower will simply take a position that can show up as either being domineering or withdrawing. There is no point in the Thinker trying to deconstruct the argument with the Knower: he will simply rationalize his position and dig his heels in further. The advice here to both parties is the same: give each other space. The Knower needs to come gently out of his dogmatism to be able to reflect and engage, and the Thinker needs to be able to reach the stage where she has processed the conflict to a degree where she can see the other's point of view. Movement by both in a compatible direction is more likely away from the heat of argument.

Feel: Know

Why is the 'heart on the sleeve' Feeler attracted to the no-fuss Knower? As I have explained, Feel can be an emotional roller coaster ride, and this is even scarier if the ride has no purpose. The Knower will bring this sense of purpose. This has some similarity to the attraction for the Thinker, but here there is a crucial difference. The attraction here is energetic. It has nothing to do with clarity. It is a feeling of magnetism. The Feeler's challenge is not that of generating energy, it is channelling it. The Knower here can be the lighthouse in the storm. Knowing is a state that naturally centers our energy. The brain and heart are collaborating, and the body is feeling confident. There are no energetic alarm bells going off in the body, as there is no sense of threat: just a sense of purpose. This effect is often described as *gravitas*. People with gravitas project energy without weakening themselves. They are a well of energy, and the Feeler will often be the first to sample the water. It can be an irresistible force.

And the Knower: why is he drawn to the Feeler? This is because the Feeler frees him from his sense of isolation. The effect is immediate and brings warmth and excitement back into his life. One of the challenges of Knowing is the tendency towards cutting off from those around you. The Feeler addresses this with a force that can penetrate the strongest fortress. Whereas the Know (primary)/Think (secondary) profile will seek the stability and pragmatism of the Thinker when he emerges from Know, the Know (primary)/Feel (secondary) profile will search out the warmth of his lover or the trust of a friend or close colleague.

And when the pressure is on? Arguments between Feelers and Knowers can be very volatile. In this state, the Feeler will pursue energy. This is high risk. The Knower will either confront or withdraw. Confrontation could escalate the energy to damaging levels. Faced by withdrawal, the Feeler will often not be able to resist pursuing her assailant. This will not solve the problem. Creating space for energy levels to subside for both parties is the most productive way ahead.

Think: Think

This pairing profile typically plays out as an orderly life for both parties. They are able to enjoy rational conversations and usually logic and pragmatism will rule the day. It is not a relationship of wild dreams or desperate lows. This pairing is all about stability and just getting on with life for what it is. When I have encountered couples with this profile they are unquestioning and workman-like in their relationship. The challenge comes when one of the pair raises their head, looks at the bigger picture and asks: "Why?"

Being so conditioned in their thinking and behavior means that they are inclined to set the bigger and more complex personal questions aside. These questions are too disruptive, and 'if it isn't broke, don't fix it' can be the attitude that prevails. Over time this approach can become less productive when the questions not being addressed are emotionally significant. Two thinkers together will sometimes lose their sense of purpose. One or both may 'wake up' one day and find that they are questioning where the relationship is going. This may have been happening over a long period, but the emotional pull is now getting so strong that it cannot be ignored. Then comes the crunch. Typically, these relationships are not well equipped to deal with major personal change. It is not that they will not get through it but more that they do not have the mindset to deal with such an uncomfortable situation.

The partner questioning the most in the relationship can be left with the choice of being open and trying to talk this through with the other partner, but he or she may not be ready. It can feel very dangerous to the relationship. So, another option is to say nothing. Unfortunately, I have experienced many people who are unhappy in relationships because they feel unable to be open about their feelings with their partner. Then there is the other unmentionable option, not always planned, which is meeting someone else. If the relationship becomes an immovable object because it is so stuck in its Think routine, it may seem easier to look outside it for excitement and change. This is fertile ground for affairs and secret encounters.

The advice is to talk it through. Be realistic in your expectations of your partner. I would suggest that the normal experience is that the emotional issues are not getting addressed and resentment simmers beneath. A typical way of us feeling better about ourselves in this situation is to look to blame the other person. Our Think profile will demand evidence, so we will go out and find all we can. This is effectively gathering ammunition. The start of the process that follows our own acknowledgment of our feelings (tough enough in itself for Thinkers) should be to look for similar signs in our partners: he or she may be feeling the same way and facing exactly the same dilemma. It may not even be that you no longer love each other; it is simply that the relationship has moved on and now its needs are different. You may both be seeking a better way.

The timing of the initial delicate discussions is, of course, crucial. If you are not addressing your emotional needs, they will eventually catch up with you, and you are in danger of them being expressed at times when they are least likely to be heard productively. Remember, if you want to have a sensitive message really heard it is critical to minimize the sense of threat: if the amygdala picks up on this you are already losing ground.

Feel: Feel

Hold on tight, as now we are really going on an emotional rollercoaster ride. As we have seen earlier, primary Feelers live off energy. They seek it in others, they offer it to you, and they can take your energy away. They can be the party animals who energize, enthuse and amuse. They love attention, not necessarily as a narcissistic need, but more to be engaged at the very center of the energy of the room. Now put two of these together in a relationship and the sparks can fly. Often the result will be a tempestuous relationship where the energy is rarely on an even keel. The highs could be shared excitement, passionate sex and adrenalin-seeking encounters that make the relationship feel alive in the moment.

Yet, of course, the reverse is also true. Energy can spiral negatively and dangerously. Arguments are likely to be confrontational and even physical. Think Richard Burton and Elizabeth Taylor. They never stopped loving each other, yet, eventually, they could not stay together. Their relationship became destructive and dangerous. Of course, we are not all Burtons and Taylors, but there are many of us playing out similar dramas behind our own closed doors.

There is another side to Feel. It can be the more internalized energy of empathy and warmth. Now the relationship dynamics change. The key to happiness here can be the simple ability to feel for the other person. Do not underestimate this. With genuine empathy comes real understanding of others. Feeling life through the position and experience of others can be the route to the happiness of both parties. When we can genuinely put ourselves in the shoes of others, we understand behaviors that previously seemed incomprehensible. Empathy is the root of forgiveness and tolerance. Instead of seeing threat to ourselves we start to see opportunity. A relationship that can share real mutual empathy is one that is blessed. There is no down-side.

Therefore, my advice to Feelers in a relationship is to enjoy the good times when you can but also to try to develop the greater sustainability of caring and empathy. Excitement has its place, but the peaks of energy must also come down and when they do where do they land? Ideally it's a safer place of quieter affection and mutual care. Primary Feel couples in this state need to work out how they regenerate their energy. If it is such a big factor in their lives, they need to be able to refill the well, not just drink from it.

Know: Know

This is a particularly fascinating relationship profile. I explained earlier that, while Knowers are usually decisive and confident people, Knowing itself is not a great relationship space. When we are in Knowing, we believe in ourselves and are convinced we have the answer. This necessarily means that Knowers do not easily get distracted by others. They remain centered by their own convictions, whether they are actually right or not. Professional athletes have to access Knowing ('the zone') if they are to reach peak performance. It is the time above all when the total body knows what is required of it and feels able to deliver. All this is impressive, but where is the room for the relationship? Surely, successful relationships are about addressing the needs of both parties. Does this mean that this pairing is doomed to failure?

This problem intrigued me for some time. I have worked with many Knowers and a lot of them have real relationship challenges, both in and outside of work. My curiosity was aroused further when I became aware of a number of Knowing marriages that had lasted a very long time, that is, 40 years plus – surely a contradiction? Of course, the propensity to marry or divorce is a wider issue with huge generational influences on people's decisions to stay or go. But I was intrigued to understand what the conditions of longevity of marriage were for these couples. I believe my answer to be valid whether we are discussing marriages or any other type of Know-to-Know relationship. Its best chance of survival is mutual respect for each other's personal space.

The older generation's marriages often survived on the basis that Dad was happy in his space and Mom was happy in hers. Typically, this may have been Dad in the shed and Mom in the kitchen. Not for a moment am I endorsing gender stereotypes here. I am not saying that these typecast roles were right, but they could work if Mom was happy to be in the kitchen and Dad was happy in the shed. It could only work if they accepted the boundaries, not if they resented them. This then evolved as Dad having a career and Mom looking after the kids. More recently, these boundaries have been blurred. The point here is not what the boundaries should be: this is a matter for every relationship to decide, and no one else has the right to pronounce what is right or wrong. The key is that they are acknowledged and agreed. So, if Mom is now in the shed and Dad is in the kitchen, that's brilliant, as long as it is what each of them wants. Knowers need their private space to be uncluttered. If they can reach an agreement, explicit or implied, that acknowledges this for both parties, then they have found a platform for continued success.

Of course, these very brief examples of using the Think Feel Know model to understand the dynamics of relationships only scratch the surface, but I hope they offer you some valuable insights. When I am coaching I take all three styles into account, and we look at the primary, secondary and other styles and how they interact across the relationship. The insight can be very powerful for my clients. The connection is usually very quick. This is not a model that needs huge processing time. It is largely intuitive and easy to understand.

I was reminded of this recently when I re-engaged with a client who had experienced one of my Think Feel Know relationship explanations. I was quite taken aback when she explained the effect it had on her and her husband. In this case, my client's primary profile was Feel and her husband's was Think. She told me that hearing my explanation had enabled her at last to work out what was going wrong in her marriage. After an extended period of heartache, she was now clear. That evening she went home to her husband and suggested that they separate. This worried me at first, as I am not in the business of breaking up relationships. I asked how she was now feeling, nine months after the separation. She said she felt "alive again". I asked how her husband was feeling (expecting the worst), but she said he also felt better than he had done for years. Now I was feeling a lot more comfortable. It was gratifying to know that both had felt relieved from the burden of trying to maintain a relationship that was no longer working.

I am not encouraging any reader to rush out and do anything impetuous. What I do hope is that I can offer you the non-judgmental language of Think Feel Know as a great basis for sharing dialog. The better the dialog and mutual understanding, the better the choices available. We can allow the differences in our styles to divide us, or we can choose to allow them to complete us.

Gender differences

"A friend is a person with whom I may be sincere.
Before him I may think aloud."

—Ralph Waldo Emerson, essayist, lecturer and poet
(1803-1882)

Before leaving this section I would like to refer to anthropology to explain some of the differences between male and female brains. It is not that the brains of the sexes are completely different or that they fall neatly into two distinct types, but there are differences in the way their physiologies have evolved that can help to explain some of the variations of behavior patterns we see on an everyday basis. I must emphasize that these are patterns, and individuals will conform to varying degrees. Some women have brains that are physiologically more 'masculine', and some men have brains that are more 'feminine'. Nevertheless, looking at their evolutionary development can offer some useful insights.

The fundamental blueprint for the development of our brains was created in the tens of thousands of years when we wandered the plains as Stone Age men and women. It was a hazardous world where humans had to face daily threats to their physical survival, be it predators or starvation. From the earliest time, the masculine body leant itself more towards the very physical demands of hunting while the female body, already cast in the role of mother, fine-tuned its ability to cope with the demands of its immediate environment. So men continued to develop as hunters, and this meant developing brains that were more specialized in spatial skills and targeting their prey. One consequence is that male brains became more likely to be focused on single-targeted activities (catching dinner) whereas female brains developed the more varied tasks of looking after the family 'nest'. The woman's job was to protect their offspring within the immediate environment in which the children would either survive or die. She was constantly tuned into sensing small movements such as those of a snake or a poisonous spider. From the earliest times she was better equipped to deal with her immediate surroundings and to multitask, with all the demands made on her.

Let's look at this with some examples of typical gender behavior today. Man goes to the fridge and looks for something woman has told him is there. Man does not see the something and returns to woman saying with total conviction that it is not there. Woman goes to same fridge and spots it immediately. How does this happen with such regularity? When man looks into the fridge his attention works like the beam of a torch, and if his torch shines on the target he will find it, but if it doesn't, he will believe it is not there. Woman's ray of attention works more like a light going on in a room. The scope of her vision is typically of a wider reach and quality and she is therefore much more likely to spot the required item.

This 'disadvantage' also gets man into trouble in other circumstances. When man walks down the street with his partner and there is an attractive female walking towards him, he cannot help but notice her. His genetic programming gives him no choice in the matter. He is 'hard-wired' to spot likely successful carriers of his genes. Socially, he has learned that to express this genetic inclination is likely to get him into big trouble once he has committed to a life partner. So, although the instinct is never completely squashed, the rules he has learned through the cortex will catch man's sexual instinct very quickly. But not always quickly enough. Man has made the mistake of turning his head ever so slightly to savour the very brief moment of gender attraction as the attractive lady passes by. Woman, being blessed with a superior field of vision, spots the slight movement of man's head. Man can now prepare for big trouble.

To make the complete unfairness of this situation even worse, woman is able to spot attractive males coming towards her without turning her head. So not only can she enjoy the glimpse of a passing male that little bit longer, she also has the satisfaction that man has no idea what she has just done.

Man's hunting history has meant that he has spent much time alone or with a small close-knit group of other hunters. He is therefore more inclined towards expressing himself through fewer words, as there was often no one else to share his thoughts and feelings with. He therefore typically uses fewer words in a day than woman. Man considers this a strength: why waste energy using more words than are really needed? Woman, however, has been used to the hustle and bustle of the family nest and likes to engage fully in all the words that are available. For her, brevity is not a strength. So, when man runs out of words or grunts, woman still has plenty of word capacity available and is not impressed by man. Man just wants to get home from a hard day's hunting and stare into the fire (in modern days called the television). Man can once again prepare for big trouble.

So, it appears that woman's claim to multitasking prowess actually has some basis in fact, although I am not sure that it is always put to the best use. When I see my daughters excitedly talking to their friends I am amazed at the way they talk over each other at top speed and yet, somehow, appear to understand one another. We poor males are resigned to looking on in wonder.

Client snapshot

Gail – where the heart is

Unlike the corporate characters above, Gail worked in a small business. She was essentially an entrepreneur. I always enjoyed the time I gave to entrepreneurs, as I found them energetic and engaging. Small businesses are much more the world of hopes and dreams. Entrepreneurs are typically people on a mission, whether that is simply about making money or about making the most of their talent.

Their personality and passion is a key ingredient of their success. They are typically pursuing a dream. Not that it makes it any easier than the corporate world, just different. Along with the hopes and energy can come disappointment and anxiety. The risk profile is typically higher, although that brings with it the opportunity for accelerated success.

Gail's story was typical of the entrepreneurs I coached. Her initial business had been set up some time ago and had achieved reasonable success. Achievement of this success had been one of the driving forces in her life since she had started the business journey. Having got there, however, she found the destination to be much less fulfilling than she had envisaged. For her, like so many others, this chapter of her career had been about proving herself, not only to others but also to herself. She had proven she was capable of developing a business idea, running with it and establishing a business around it – something to be genuinely proud of. Yet now she was feeling lost.

Proving ourselves and what we are capable of can be a very powerful motivator as we construct our career and business. It can keep us focused and committed. Yet, as this case shows, the destination can be disappointing. Typically the factors that have driven and influenced our motivation have moved on. What we want from life has evolved. Gail's primary style was Know/Feel and the lack of a sense of current purpose was affecting her personal life and her business. Our coaching conversations were therefore all about re-engaging with what really mattered to her, not just in business but in life in general.

She held very strong beliefs and values. Until now she had dealt with her personal dreams as something quite apart from the business. She harbored the ambition to do something of much greater social value, specifically around supporting mothers in childbirth in developing nations. Her thinking was based on the famous notion of 'one-day': "One day I will be able to turn my attention from the business to the stuff that I really want to do." It is not uncommon to come across this mindset. And while it may work temporarily, over time the gap between compliance to business requirements and commitment to a real sense of personal value becomes wider. The business was now largely draining her, both emotionally and financially.

Our discussions were therefore about reframing her perspective on the balance between business and non-business life. Over time it was about understanding what she really wanted her life to be about. Then we were able to discuss scenarios for creating the connection between her business and her wider personal life ambition. By aligning these needs she would be able to breathe revitalized life and energy into both. They could become mutually supportive rather than competing for her energy. If we understand the source of our energy and plug into it, there is more than enough to support us. It cannot be easily compartmentalized into separate boxes. In terms of the Think/Feel/Know styles, thinkers are the best at doing this compartmentalization, and Gail was certainly no Thinker. Yet even those with the strongest Think profiles will eventually need to connect with their source of energy and their sense of purpose.

Teams

*"We may have all come on different ships,
but we're in the same boat now."*

—Martin Luther King, Jr. (1929-1968)

Let's now look at how Think Feel Know profiling applies at
the team level.

Business

*"Success is not final, failure is not fatal:
it is the courage to continue that counts."*

—Winston Churchill (1874-1965)

I have done a lot of coaching with senior business and
leadership teams. The normal experience, as I become
engaged with a new client, is that I start off working with
the business leader, for example the CEO, and when the time
is right the CEO will ask me to engage with his or her team.
Typically, we work together on the strategic development of
the business, particularly the people aspects, core to which
is the functioning of the top team, especially relationships
within and across the team.

Far from being soft and fluffy stuff, my many years of business
experience have taught me that successful relationships
sit at the heart of all business success. Nobody can achieve
sustainable success on their own. We all need people to
support us and work with us, whether it is internal colleagues,
clients or partners. Yet my experience has also taught me that
leadership and management teams are generally not teams
at all. They are groups of people whose job responsibilities

mean that they have to meet in order to achieve some level of team co-ordination. The team leader will, of course, do his best to maintain a semblance of teamwork and will try hard to keep team members all on the same track, but typically, as soon as the team meeting is over, each member will revert to his own agenda, and that will normally mean alliances with some colleagues and also competition and even conflict with others.

The reality is that most team members are career competitors, and they cannot all get the boss's job. So, while the corporate ideal may be one of leadership teams riding off together into the sunset, the everyday experience is a much more complex tapestry of personal agendas and career ambitions mixed with a constant tension between occasional collaborative intent and inevitable competition. I am not for a moment judging corporate business people negatively here. I am convinced that most of us share the craving for a genuine environment of shared trust where we can feel valued by our peers. My negative judgment is actually about the corporate environment we have created that makes such open and trusting behavior a high-risk personal strategy. The business world is an example of the modern-day jungle where the human instinct for personal survival will never be far below the surface, and if that means survival at the expense of colleagues, then so be it.

It amazes me how so much management theory ignores this basic observation. It is as though all we need is someone to sound the rallying call and we will all start turning up ready and willing to die for the team. This could not be further from the truth. More likely the assembled troops will arrive expecting the worst and with their antennae highly tuned to spot any threat. We need only revert to the neurological principles we covered earlier. The brain is geared first and foremost to be wary of threat, and corporate change is normally seen as threatening. Of course, experienced corporate business people – and I confess myself to have been included in this category – have become very skilled in the appearance of teamwork, so to the untrained eye it may seem like we are committed. Yet, in most cases, the best you can hope for is compliance. Compliance is the world of publically observable behavior; commitment is about feelings and giving what we want to give.

I will return to this challenge later when we will look at advanced performance, but for now I hope this has reinforced how critical it is to address the reality of top team working if you want to run a sustainably successful business. And what matters most in the top team dynamic is not either strategy or operation (both of which have their place) it is the emotions that are shared within that team. If the team is positively emotionally engaged and aligned with the challenge it will create authentic space to develop strategy and operation. Without such emotional engagement, strategy and operation are little more than a set of tasks that will be delivered with compliance and negotiation. The true capability of human commitment will, however, be left in the file of 'missed opportunities'

Client snapshot

David – the good guy

David is a great example of a good guy who was never given the right chance in the corporate environment. He had worked his way up the corporate ladder at a steady pace. He was blessed with a good intellect and excellent people skills. People liked working for him because he cared for them. He was very committed to achieving business results but did so through his people rather than in spite of them. On the other hand, it is fair to say that he did not always *demonstrate the clinical behavior sometimes demanded by his bosses and this held up his career to some degree.*

Eventually, he did get the opportunity to lead at a business divisional level. The people that had appointed him had recognized that his rounded skill-set could be crucial in pulling together a fractious culture. David was very balanced across the Think, Feel, Know profiles. He could operate comfortably in each of the styles. We were working on strengthening his Knowing behavior, which meant in his case staying connected with his sense of purpose and communicating it to his people. This was undoubtedly improving. Yet, having appointed him to the role, the organization did nothing to support him. He was dropped in like a paratrooper behind enemy lines in the hope that he would change the flow of the conflict. And, of course, it would have taken a superhuman effort to have achieved this. The instincts behind the initial appointment were good, but they were not carried through. Just over a year after his appointment he left the organization.

David always recognized that he had taken on a difficult challenge and never regretted doing so. It proved to be an excellent learning experience for him, if not always an enjoyable one. The prime reason we were working on his Knowing style was that this was the behavior demanded by the organization. It was a very macho culture, and if you weren't seen to be tough, you weren't seen at all.

The corporate world is often a world of short-term results, and people and culture change do not follow these rules. Relationships need time. When the pressure increased in this business, they resorted to the normal response: get someone else in. Given time, people like David can change cultures, but they cannot swim against the tide of corporate conditioning.

It therefore makes a great deal of sense to start team coaching by looking at the relationships within the team, and communication styles and preferences sit at the heart of this team dynamic.

Applying Think Feel Know profiling techniques to team working follows the same principles as those used in pairing relationships but now we look across the total team. While an online profiling tool is available, I also like to get team members to profile one another. Of course, this has to be done at the right time, when the Think Feel Know model has been fully explained and when there is sufficient trust in the room for permission to be given for the mutual profiling to proceed. The beauty of this approach, as indeed with all physiologically based explanation, is that it removes peer judgment. It is a lot more constructive to feed back to a colleague how you experience her communication and behavioral style in the language of Thinking, Feeling and Knowing than is it to rate her on a comparative scale, where her immediate response will be to feel threatened.

Equally, this feedback does not 'pigeonhole' her. There will be contradictions in how colleagues feed back data. This does not invalidate the feedback in any way. It is perfectly understandable that some colleagues will view their peers differently to others: this could be a reflection of any number of variables, including the time they spend together, the type of job responsibilities each one has, geography or the relationships they have built to date. What matters is not the absolute accuracy of the Think Feel Know classification itself but the conversation that then should follow. Opportunities for business people to share honest, constructive feedback about their respective styles and behavior are precious and rare. In fact, they are often avoided because people feel they don't have the skills or the working environment to take on such a 'delicate' discussion. So, creating opportunities within the team coaching environment for team members to share one another's perspectives in this way can be insightful, powerful and are an essential platform for team building.

So let's look at some real examples of team profiles I have worked with, again anonymously of course, and discuss the implications arising. In the three cases below, each team member was asked to present his or her view of the profile of each of his or her team colleagues by using the classification Think (T), Feel (F) or Know (K). They were asked to answer which was the primary style (the style used the most frequently), the secondary style (the second most frequent) and the 'other' style (used the least). The profiles shown for each team member are the average view of the team. Sometimes this was very clear cut. At other times it was a closer call. I did not use the team member's own view of his or her own profiles: this was a point of interest and conversation, but for this exercise it was more relevant to look at how they 'showed up' to the team.

Business 1

This was a corporate team leading a large global telecoms business. There were six key members of the team and they agreed their profiles to be:

Style	Individuals						Team
	A	B	C	D	E	F	
Primary	T	T	K	T	K	T	T
Secondary	F	F	T	F	T	K	K
Other	K	K	F	K	F	F	F

I would encourage you here to look at the profile yourself and to think about some of the possible implications arising before reading on.

First, a note of caution: two teams sharing the same profile does not mean they face the same issues. The profiling is rather a vehicle for getting the right issues on the table without all the personal judgment that normally goes with team feedback. This is a constructive way of registering what behaviors may be limiting the team's progress without blaming it on any particular individual team member. Responsibility remains collective, and what matters now is deciding how they move forward, not how the blockages may have arisen in the first place.

So, what was the main challenge for the team above? Well, you can see that the team's primary strength is Think. Unsurprising perhaps in what was essentially a technical business. They were strong at analysis, methodology and problem-solving. This primary talent was mixed across the team with two Knowers. This is helpful for forcing decisions on issues. Knowers do not like to get lost in the detail: so far, so good. The challenge was the apparent absence of Feel. The consequence of this was that the team could be experienced as somewhat robotic and lacking in human empathy. They could deal with one another in this same workman-like way. They would not naturally find time for investing in relationships, both within the team and as a general approach to their leadership of their business. This does not mean they never found time, but it was generally lower down the list. It would also seem that they were probably missing opportunities to engage and motivate their people.

In agreeing this data and exploring the conversation around it, the team readily and willingly concluded that this needed to be addressed. It made sense of some of the challenges they had created for themselves. They therefore resolved to create a better behavioral balance in the team, allowing more Feel time at the top table where relationship and cultural challenges could be acknowledged and discussed constructively rather than being swept under the carpet or left to fester until the blister burst. Having three team members with Feel as their secondary style meant that they were well positioned to achieve this.

Business 2

This was a mid-size business operating nationally throughout the United Kingdom. Here the agreed team profile was:

Style	Individuals						Team
	A	B	C	D	E	F	
Primary	K	K	T	T	F	K	K
Secondary	F	F	F	K	T	T	T
Other	T	T	K	F	K	F	F

Here we have a team with a primary Know profile. This means that they took no prisoners and very quickly got things done. Think was their secondary style, marginally ahead of Feel. On first examination, you may conclude that this is a good dynamic mix where decisions get made, supported with due analysis and consideration. There were times when this was undoubtedly true. Equally true is the observation that the Knowers were so strong in the team that the rest of the team got left behind.

This was a 'macho' environment where you either got into the battle and fought your corner or you were ignored. It was made worse by the fact that all the Knowers were male and the others were female. So, lots of testosterone-filled meetings were the order of the day where the alpha males fought to defend or improve their position in the team. Sometimes these meetings were brilliant; sometimes they became dysfunctional. Occasionally, the Knower/Feelers would let their feelings out, constructively or destructively, while The Knower/Thinker would stick to a more deliberate and controlled plan to try to play the longer game. The bottom-line is that they were not really operating as a team. Management meetings were an arena where the gladiatorial contest could take place, and the Christians knew there was always a danger of them being thrown to the lions.

Examining this agreed data was the first step for the team to really come to terms with what was going on. It gave the Knowers the opportunity to reflect and agree on what they could do to make themselves more accessible to the rest of the team. The non-Knowers felt they had been acknowledged. They had more to offer than spectatorship, and this experience was giving them a rare opportunity to register the frustrations without the lions straining at their leashes.

Business 3

This was a corporate business where the leadership team consisted of five main team members. Their agreed profile was:

Style	Individuals					Team
	A	*B*	*C*	*D*	*E*	
Primary	T	F	T	K	F	T/F
Secondary	K	T	K	F	K	
Other	F	K	F	T	T	K

In this case, there was not a decisive primary team style. They were very inclined towards both Think and Feel, and this meant that they operated very rationally and methodically, but they were also quite an engaging team with good relationships both within the team and with key stakeholders. And their challenge? It was the lack of primary Know and the most likely consequence of this can be a slowness to commit and to make decisions. The sole primary Knower in the team was not in an appropriate job position to make decisions on behalf of the team as a whole, so this provided no solution.

This first analysis was partly valid but, as always, the reality was more subtle. In fact, three members of the team had Know as their secondary style and therefore were quite comfortable about making decisions if the need arose. However, they were missing opportunities to project themselves in a truly decisive way. Think Feel Know data is first about communication and behavioral style. This team was inevitably cast in a role of leadership, and they were not always taking opportunities to project themselves in a leadership light. People in the rest of their organization needed to know where they stood on key issues. They needed to know where the business was going and what the future held.

Our conversations therefore focused on this leadership challenge, the need to establish a clear strategic vision and purpose for the business and the need to create the motivational connection for their people to feel they wanted to commit to the journey. Actually, as a team, they had all the key ingredients to succeed. It was more a case of upping their awareness of the need to lead from the front and teasing out of them the modifications in behavioral style each one of them was capable of in order to support this aim. It was a simple message and one to which they responded with great enthusiasm. They had great talent and were great people; they just needed to be better at communicating this.

These are three simple cases of real teams that show how the profiling data can be used to support learning. I have worked with many leadership teams, and, as you would expect, they come in many varied shapes and sizes. The main principles are clear: the team needs to have sufficient access to each of the Think, Feel and Know talents if it is to enjoy sustainable success. Additionally, team members need to be seen first as people, not living-job-descriptions. All too often, senior managers are cast too rigidly in the prescriptive requirements of their job descriptions and this can result in opportunities being lost to encourage them to contribute as people, with all the width and depth of talent they can bring with them.

A team that is over-dependent on Think will be solid and reliable but could also be ponderous and rigid. A team that is over-dependent on Feel is likely to swing between excited and depressed. A team of Knowers will not be a team. As individuals they will be driven, convincing and decisive but they will carve up the territory in whatever way they can get away with. It is no coincidence that one of the most common challenges I am asked to support my clients in addressing in the corporate world is that of 'silo behavior', where loyalty in the business sits with the parts rather than the whole. The unforgiving world of corporate business has itself encouraged Knowing behavior, the struggle for survival and the survival of the 'fittest'. Hardly surprising then that it should find itself deeply entrenched in the territorial combat of silo warfare.

In all of these cases, getting teams to agree their profiles can prove very useful in allowing them to move to a better level of collective performance. Nevertheless, I trust it also demonstrates that this is only support data. The data still has to be used with wisdom and by skilful practitioners. Mechanical use of psychometric data devalues the complexity of human behavior and blurs the rich tapestry of our potential.

The data provokes and supports valuable conversations: it does not replace them.

Sport

"We must learn to live together as brothers or perish together as fools."

—Martin Luther King, Jr. (1929-1968)

While most of my team coaching has been conducted within businesses, I have also been involved occasionally with sport. At the professional level this was in football and in golf. Of course, my coaching was not about the technicalities of the game (if you saw me playing golf that would be self-evident) it was more about the psychological and emotional aspects. Sport has always been an important part of my life as participant and spectator, and I have always found these assignments very enjoyable. Having said this, they have typically been of a limited nature, for example working with a team for a short period or running workshops.

So, when the opportunity came to work with a football team over a full season I was intrigued to see how my coaching work could be carried through to match days. I have included this story in this book because I believe the principles of team performance are largely the same in both sport and business. Of course, there are differences at the application level, but the fundamentals are the same. I would encourage any business readers to keep this actively in mind when reading the next few pages. This could just as easily be a story about a CEO and his leadership team.

The opportunity came when I was approached by the manager of a football club (known here as D) to support him in managing the team's quest for promotion. The team had a long history of 108 years in football, but the division 1 championship had always eluded them. The manager had achieved good success over the last two seasons, and the team finished sixth in the division, but he felt that something else was needed to find that last crucial element for greater success. Additionally, he wanted personal support in supporting his own style of management. His reputation was excellent, having been successful as a footballer himself in his younger days. He was known to be passionate, committed and fair, so he had no difficulty in attracting good footballers to his club. The challenge for him was that his passion could become so intense that he became intimidating. His Knowing style gave him the sense of purpose and the vision, and his sense of fun energized his players: all well and good when things were going to plan, but not so good when they were not.

From the first game I watched, it was clear that his team were playing under pressure. They were good footballers, but they did not seem to be playing with the freedom and expression their talent deserved. It was as though the players were more concerned about not making mistakes than really going all out for success. The manager himself was very animated in the 'dug-out' but far too much of his behavior was negative. His own emotions were getting the better of him, and this was affecting the team. It was not that the players disliked him; it was more that they couldn't handle him in this state.

The manager was a clever guy. My guess is that intuitively he knew what was going on – hence the request for help, but it can be difficult to acknowledge the issue when you do not know how you can resolve it. So D and I set out on discussions to agree how both he and the team could be best supported. We agreed two parallel tracks: first, to support D to learn to modify his behavior and, second, to support the players to play more confidently as a team.

He was an excellent client. We built mutual trust quickly, and he was always open to feedback and suggestions. On match days I would be nearby, simply making the occasional comment or gesture to remind him to keep his comments positive and supportive. Don't get me wrong, if players are not trying their best harsh words may be appropriate, but this should be a considered judgment based on having the right impact, not simply a spill-over from the manager's own inability to contain his emotions. And slowly, but surely, he did modify his style.

The personal engagement with the manager was classic one-to-one coaching, albeit in a sporting environment. And without his obvious support it would not have been possible to have any affect on the players. The engagement with the players was especially interesting for me, providing a new challenge and a valuable learning opportunity. In the early days it was just a matter of letting the players get used to seeing me in the dressing room and on match days. Slowly I was able to build some rapport with key players, get to know them and learn to 'speak their language'. I wanted to explain the science of human performance to them, but they were not a traditional audience. So everything I explained had to be in footballing terms, or at least in terms they could relate to. It was fascinating for me to see early skepticism slowly evolve into acceptance and even enthusiasm.

I had to manage the relationships within the team very carefully. Every dressing room has its key influencers, and it was vital for me to get them on my side. In general, the younger lads were more open and enthusiastic and would have no problem in coming to me for personal chats, especially if their form was suffering or if they had not been selected to play. This was more of a challenge for the older guys. They did not have their footballing careers in front of them like their younger team-mates and their footballing lessons were already clearly laid down in the tracks of their memory. The 'stuff' I was talking about could sound weird and fanciful if expressed wrongly. And, of course, it was vital that I did not take myself too seriously. Being able to handle dressing room banter and humor was all a critical part of the acceptance process. Equally, I had to sense when I had to stand my ground.

Eventually it was the older guys in the team that did my talking for me. They became the role models for what I was trying to communicate. Although they would not share my language, they agreed completely with the principles I explained. This was the source of the real change that went on in the dressing room. The senior players would always be more directly influential than me, but when we aligned our talents, sometimes unconsciously, really good things started to happen.

So, let's look a little closer at how I used the science and the Think Feel Know model to support the team.

Think

In terms of team football, the Think element is all about the planning and preparation that goes on before the game. It runs right through the club and includes attention to the detail of the things that matter. It includes any intelligence that can be built about the opponents and the totality of the fitness and training regime that players are expected to follow. It includes the patterns of play that are rehearsed on the training ground, and it certainly includes the tactical plans that are hatched for the match.

A great deal of the available time was put into thinking about which players fitted best into which position, bearing in mind the expected approach of the opponents. Of course, our team had to play to its own strengths, but the manager would always try to balance this with the anticipated threat posed by the particular opposition. The tactical plan provided the essential platform for team performance. Everyone needed clarity about their position and how they were expected to perform on the day.

When matches were not going our way, and there will always be matches that don't go your way (or at least times in those matches that don't go your way), the fall-back was always 'stick to the plan'. It provides the essential basis for regrouping because it is the point of understanding that everyone in the team shares. It should therefore be the team's safety net and because of this no one was allowed to change the plan other than the manager. Players who took it on themselves to walk away from the plan and do their own thing would cause chaos in the team. As soon as one player strays into the role of another player that other player has to change his own plan in order to accommodate the change of circumstances. Now we have two players not playing to the plan, and so on it goes until there is no plan, and teams without a plan do not win football matches at professional levels.

At this point, this may start to look like a rather robotic approach to football. What about flair and creativity? Of course, these are just as essential, but they are not Think. Note, I said that teams without a plan do not win matches. I did not say that plans alone will ensure a win. It takes more. But the Think element provides the foundation for the performance.

Feel

The Feel element is where practice makes perfect. Constant practice fine-tunes the operation of the motor neural system as players literally get the feel for their art. Here learning is done through sensing, not by logic. Nothing can teach you logically about the touch of the ball or the weighting of a pass; it is something you have to experience. The body is engaged, and the senses are key to this engagement. Of course, others can help you learn techniques so you know the rules to follow (the cortex), but you can only master your art by applying these techniques in the way that works best for you. You are the only person in the world with your body, your experiences and your emotions. Feel is a very personal world.

In Feel, we are also entering the world of 'form' as it is often called in sporting terms. Being in good form generally means that you are playing well and using your talents successfully at that time. Yet, as all sporting enthusiasts know, form can be very temporary. It can disappear in the blink of an eye. This is because it is directly connected with the way we feel about ourselves in the moment and about our ability to use our talents successfully. We can have a great plan, and we can have mastered our skills to the highest level, but if we do not feel good at the crucial moment then our performance will suffer. This is because the radar device in the brain, the amygdala, is sensing threat. Something has happened immediately beforehand, or there has been a slow build-up of uncertainty. This creates fearful images in the brain. When threat is expected, energy is sent to all parts of the body to fend off attack. This is wasted energy and distraction. Instead of focusing positively on the task in hand our perspective becomes cluttered and our emotions volatile. The body is caught in the tension between performance and threat.

So a key part of providing coaching support to individual players is supporting them to feel good about themselves at the time they need it most. And this cannot be superficial commentary. No one will be convinced by clichés and empty phrases. It is about understanding how they really feel about themselves, what makes them feel great and what blockages can get in the way. Maintaining positive feelings in the days building up to the game is probably more about their lives in general and will involve as much off-the-field considerations as those on it. On match day, however, it has to focus on what is good about being in the field of play. There may be other areas that make the footballer feel good outside his sport, but he needs to keep his concentration focused on the game, so helping the player to create and sustain his own positive and relevant emotional state in the field of play is crucial.

So, there is a vital individual element to the Feel dimension of football, but what about the team aspect? This is also critical and is all about the relationships within the team. Every successful football manager will know how important relationships are in the dressing room and on the field of play. Players have to want to play with one another. They need to go out on to the pitch knowing that they can trust their team-mates and feeling that the team is more important than any one individual. It seems straightforward but it is not: it needs work. Team sport is a complex mix of individual and team ambitions. Every player wants to be part of a successful team and also wants to be a key player within it. So the ideal scenario for each player is indisputable – a winning team performance and an excellent personal performance. Beyond that, it is less clear. If the player was given the choice between a good personal performance and a good team performance (that is he can only claim one or the other, not both) he will probably say that it is all about the team, especially if his team-mates are listening. Yet the feelings of personal disappointment and anxiety are the strongest feelings he will take home with him after a poor personal performance.

Getting players to understand the energetic dimension of feelings is very valuable. They 'get it'. They know all about the energetic effect a crowd can have on them. I have talked to players at professional football clubs and stood on the touchline before big games. The intensity of the energy does not truly come across on television. Yes, you can hear the noise, but players directly feel the energy. They can pick up individual remarks among the wall of noise. They can sometimes see the faces of those who adore or hate them. They can attack their opponents with the home crowd lifting their pace and belief, or they can get swallowed up by the ferocity of an away crowd. Energetic transaction is a fundamental part of every sporting encounter, whether it is the feelings of the players on the day or the transmitted effect of the mass of spectators.

Client snapshot

K

Occasionally, I have taken my coaching work into other areas. Primarily these have been sporting areas, where my passion remains unbridled; worthy charities, where I wish to offer value to those who could not otherwise afford my services; and religion, where I remain fascinated by the concept of spirituality. As a complete one-off, I did some work in a prison.

The particular case in mind here was where I was running some workshops in a level two prison, which meant that I was dealing with serious offenders, including those convicted of grievous body harm (GBH) – but not convicted murderers or sex offenders. I was working in the service with those responsible for rehabilitation. The particular regime in place there rewarded positive inmate behavior with increased access to privileges like the library or the gym. If they continued to behave responsibly in the gym, the rehabilitation officer wanted to give them a further reward of additional educational insight that may help them when they were released. I agreed to help them with this for a period of time.

Naturally, walking into a prison of convicted offenders is not the same as delivering a university lecture. A key consideration for me was the choice of language and area of story-telling I would use to help them connect with principles that may not have been explained to them before in the most effective way. The rehabilitation officer and I agreed that a sport theme was likely to be the most productive area.

So, after walking through endless security points, accompanied by a designated guard at all times, and through the gym area, where I was greeted by looks that could at best be described as wary, I made my way to a venue that had been designated the workshop area. It was a predictably oppressive environment, but at least the guard was still with me and the inmates had actually turned up for the session. As I walked in there it was not so much a case of sudden silence but more one of being totally ignored. Understandably, they were going to make me work for their acceptance. The guard insisted that they turn around to face me (albeit at the furthest possible distance) and the rest was down to me.

The opening salvos from the inmates were clearly designed to test my mettle. Did I know I was in a room full of people (about 10 in total) who had been convicted for violent crimes? And there is only one guard? And how much was I getting paid to do this stuff? At this point I was glad that I was not charging a fee as I may have lost them. They may have considered me a soft touch but that was probably better than them thinking of themselves as a simple meal ticket. Gradually, the barriers dropped away as I explained to them that I was a 'valleys' boy', just as they were (that is, someone brought up in the mining valleys of South Wales), and I was just going to talk to them about sport. The choice of sport as the main metaphor running through the workshop worked extremely well. The fact that I had done some work in professional sport with personalities they readily recognized gave credence to my insights. And, of course, humor was essential. There was nothing manufactured in this. I found their comments very funny, even those directed at me.

Slowly, they started to bring their chairs forward and started to engage. One of the 'ring leaders' picked up on this and suggested that they all move up to the table; now they were sat forward, chatting and energized – with one exception. One of their number had sat side-on from me from the outset and had offered me no acknowledgment. Even when the others moved forward he stayed on the outside of the group, apparently as isolated from them as he was from me. When one of the other inmates noticed me looking at the outsider, he suggested that I should not waste my time on him as he was 'weird' (or words to that effect). Of course, I did not want to risk losing the main group so I temporarily moved on, and the individual remained stranded from the group.

As part of the workshop, I weaved in some very basic insights around how Think Feel Know works with football teams and then tried to explain communicating by Feel.

Then I noticed a book in front of our estranged inmate. All I could see on the cover was animals. So I explained Feel communication by suggesting that they consider animals. As soon as I did this, I noticed a slight change in the outsider's posture, as though he may have suddenly become interested. I explained how animals use energy, body language and noises to make themselves understood. I suggested that animals were probably better at this than humans were and that we could draw many lessons from the way they expressed their desires, excitement, authority, loyalty, sadness, fear and trust. I think I had him at 'trust'. He never quite got to sit with the other members of the group, but he did pull his chair much closer and his attention stayed with me for the rest of the session. It looked like this guy had an affinity with animals that he was not able to share with humans. He said nothing for the whole workshop, but I knew he was engaged; in keeping with his affinity, he let me know by glances, energy and posture. Sometimes we have to look beyond the obvious to connect with those who appear not to be readily accessible to us.

Know

In sporting terms, Knowing is all about being 'in the zone'. This is the targeted destination for all athletes. You cannot decide simply to go into Knowing. It is a journey that starts in Think, moves through Feel, and when these two are aligned, the door to Knowing is opened. Players in the zone make their art look so easy. This is because, in psycho-physiological terms, it is. Of course, they may be operating at incredible levels of fitness and skills, but the body knows it can handle it. When they access the zone they tap into an intuitive intelligence. They do not have to think about what they are doing, the program is already written. There is no sense of threat, no distraction and no lack of belief. In fact, 'no' does not exist. It is all about what can be done: the execution of a task done many times before and which the athlete enjoys performing. All the body's energy is focused down one channel. There is no doubt, and when the mind and body are optimized in this way, peak performance is achieved.

Sport psychologists have been working extensively with similar principles over recent times, and they are now a natural ingredient of most sporting success at the highest levels. In the earlier days, this was done rather superficially and with mixed success. Techniques such as goal visualization have been around for some time and can be very successful. More recently, the development of neurology and the access to fMRI data has helped us to understand how this works and can underpin this success still further.

So, for the individual footballers, it is about supporting them on the journey through Think and Feel and helping them to access the zone. So, how does this work on a team level? The principles are exactly the same. The team needs to plan and prepare *as a team*. They need to have a match day plan that everyone understands and sticks to. They need to feel good about one another. When these two elements come together, they are able to operate as one efficient unit, maximizing the talents of the team: the team is then in Knowing.

Match day performance

This sounds relatively straightforward. The problem is usually the opposition. If only they wouldn't mess things up. So let's look at how these Think Feel and Know principles can be played out in the heat of battle. Each plays their part.

Let's think of this in physiological terms. I explained earlier that the cortex is the area of the brain where we create the rules by which we behave, and therefore the rules by which we perform. The cortex does not operate in the moment as quickly as the limbic and basal regions do. It is therefore the place that stabilizes performance by constantly keeping it on track. The cortex seeks clarity and, if it gets it, it will act as a moderating influence on the rest of the brain. In this sense, the cortex provides the framework and the plan for the performance.

We worked hard to drum into the players the team plan for every match. It was the first thing we talked about when they arrived in the dressing room on match day and the last thing we talked about before they went out on to the pitch. The team plan was the one place where they could all meet mentally and understand one another. In the heat of sporting battle, emotions will hijack the brain and players will lose perspective and become de-stabilized. This can never be completely removed, but it can be minimized. So, when players are under pressure and can feel themselves 'losing it', they need to know what to do about it. If they don't know this the period of anxiety will extend and so will the loss of performance. If they do know they can recover quickly. So getting back to the plan was essential and served us well as an approach that the players mastered more and more as the season progressed.

This is the process of moving from Feel into Think. The volatile energy of Feel needs to be neutralized in order for all parts of the brain to be effectively re-engaged in the performance. The body needs to move from feeling threatened to feeling that it is back in control. Control starts with the cortex and happens when it is following its own tried and tested rules. The approach can be described as getting back to basics. All too often players who are struggling in a game try to do something special so that they can feel better about themselves. This rarely works. Getting back to doing the things you know you can do rather than the things you hope you can do is a much safer path to performance recovery.

From a Feel perspective, it was all about keeping everyone feeling positive about themselves, about one another and about their ability to win the match. While the Think element above provided the platform, it was the Feel dimension that inspired the players to excel. This energetic piece of the jigsaw was capable of lifting everyone to a new level of performance. When you see your team-mates doing great things, and when this is underpinned by you feeling good about yourself, you can be amazing.

Over the course of the season, we managed some very Knowing team performances. At its best, the team could just be left to get on with the job. The tactics were clear, they were feeling good and so they hardly needed any interventions from us. Players in a Knowing state bring intuitive intelligence into their conduct of the game. They used a combination of their sensing of what was going on around them and their accumulated experience to know when to drive the team forward and when to settle the team down. The fundamentals of the plan did not change, as this was only within the remit of the manager, but confident players know how to work the plan to best effect. The relationship between the manager and the captain is crucial here. The manager has the advantage of seeing the total game from the outside: the captain is in the middle of the action and knows how the game feels. If these two communicate effectively (recognizing that most of this communication itself has to be by gesture and intuitive connection) it can be a huge bonus for the team.

By the time I was fully integrated into the football team, we had changed the match day routine. After all the physical preparation had been done and the tactical discussions concluded, we would spend the last few minutes before going out to the game in the dressing room in silence. This was a time for each player to collect his thoughts and feelings and channel them for the game. No eye contact was allowed with other players as this would only serve as a distraction. Some players would look firmly at the floor, and others would put their shirts over their heads. This was their time to be at ease with the challenge ahead, to remember why they loved the game so much and to carry with them all the good things they were capable of. For me, this is a metaphor for life.

On the other hand, it is not realistic to expect to be in a positive emotional state throughout every match, all season, and the team will be tested when results do not go to plan. I have a particular memory of a very important game against one of our key rivals. We had prepared everything in the normal way and had set out a plan that we believed would succeed. With 10 minutes remaining in the game, we were winning by three goals to one, and we had already proved over the season what a difficult team we were to beat, conceding an average of less than one goal per game. All was going to plan, and the championship ambition was moving closer. Yet, when the final whistle blew to close the game, we had lost five goals to three. The turn-around in the game was incredible. One moment we were in complete control and were playing a beaten team. The next moment we conceded a second goal, and one of our key players was injured in the process, and the whole nature of the game was energetically transformed. The opponents suddenly believed they could win and so did their home crowd. Energetically, we could not cope. We conceded four goals in 10 minutes.

After the game, the dressing room was like a morgue. We knew we had let a crucial opportunity slip, and we could not really understand why. This was a critical test for the team, a defining moment. It would have been so easy to slip into recrimination and regret, and I suspect the same manager of the previous season may have done exactly that. That could have cost us the season. Yet we all knew that everyone had tried their best. Nobody could be faulted for effort. We were in a state of shock. Superficial positivity would not work. The players were hurting too much. Denial of the pain was not going to help here. So, we just had to allow the pain to sink in and allow each player to process it in his own way. We never really spent any serious time analyzing what had gone wrong: we just put it down to 'one of those things'. This may sound superficial, but it served to remind the players that whatever we do to prepare for a game we are never totally in control. All we can do is give our best, work hard for one another, enjoy one another's company and remain totally committed and vigilant when we are in the field of play. If we look after these things, then, mostly, the results will look after themselves.

Ironically, this proved to be the final making of our season. From there we went through the rest of the season without losing another game and eventually ran out champions for the first time in the club's long history. So, how much did this type of coaching support contribute to this success? The truth is that it is hard to separate from all the other ingredients. The right mental and emotional approach to the game cannot be a substitute for talent and fitness; on the other hand, the science proves just how dependent we are on our emotional state. In the search for excellence over and above our competitors an extra five to 10% of performance derived from Thinking, Feeling and Knowing alignment can make the difference between being at the top of the tree or just being one of the branches.

Translating to business

I invite you to read or at least scan the last section on the sports team again. The principles are exactly the same as in business. The Think, Feel and Know dimensions will play out in precisely the same way. Think of your own business team, whether you are leading it or are a team member. To develop the parallel, think that your team is not always in play. Each person has their own down time away from the team, whether it is personal preparation, other responsibilities or private matters. Be clear about when the team is in play and what your plan is for these occasions.

In Think terms, every business team needs clarity about its way of playing and who is playing in each position (job roles). How do these roles fit together so that each member of the team can be clear about how you will cover the field of play? Each player has to have the requisite level of technical competence to be able to succeed at this level. Each member needs to feel confident about how each of his team-mates will interpret his role in match play. What are team tactics? A team without a clear shared understanding of its tactical (operational) plan is a team that will splinter under pressure. The team plan must be the platform of team cohesion.

In Feel terms, what are you doing as a team to invest in relationships? This is too important to leave to chance. Players who do not want to work together will always find the team agenda challenging. Your team meetings are the dressing room before the game. Building and maintaining effective working team relationships has to be as important a commitment as your operational plan.

Get the above two factors right and your team will be ready to move into Knowing. The final step is creating the vision that aligns the team and energizes each member. In my football example, our vision was clear: it was to win the championship. All visions need three critical ingredients: they need to be understandable (Think), energizing (Feel) and believable (Know). Our vision ticked all three boxes and every squad member felt a part of trying to achieve it. What is the vision for your team? What is the shared sense of purpose that motivates the team to work through the sweat and pain of training so that they are equipped to deserve their place in the field of play? What inspires them to perform? There is no greater celebration than one you can genuinely share with those who made it happen.

When a team moves into Knowing, it is performing at its most optimal. No need for slowing up and checking the rules, no difficult relationships and no fear of failure – just a clear understanding of what each of their team-mates is doing, a desire to want to work together and a decisive belief that they can succeed.

Organizational culture

"I've learned that people will forget what you said, people will forget what you did, but people will never forget how you made them feel."

—Maya Angelou, American author and poet (1928-)

Defining culture

Having dealt with individuals and teams, the next step is to look at organizations. Virtually every business I have worked with has recognized and expressed the need to deal with cultural challenges but few report positively on the progress they have made. It would appear that organizational culture is like a jelly. When you prod it, it will change shape with the pressure of your finger, but as soon as the finger is removed it returns to its usual shape. The challenge of sustainable cultural change appears to be elusive to many organizations.

Real behavior change is very difficult to achieve. We can pursue compliance via rules, processes, authority structures and job descriptions, but none of these can offer the flexibility and openness of behavior that many organizations crave in today's increasingly fast-moving business environment.

So what do we mean by culture? There are many definitions available, but I will offer you my own. For me, the culture of an organization is simply the aggregate effect of all the relationships within that organization. Relationships are about feelings and feelings are about energy.

Organizational culture has nothing directly to do with plans, processes, structures, projects, job descriptions or procedures. You cannot think your way to culture change. Traditionally in business, we retreat when it comes to the world of feelings and emotions. This is the soft and fluffy stuff that hard-headed business people would prefer to set aside. My generation was told to 'leave their feelings at home' when they came to work. Yet, we know that feelings are essential to successful relationships, and without these relationships, we cannot have a sustainable business.

The difficulty is that there is no set of readily available rules that can be applied in the good old logical problem-solving sense to get this stuff resolved. I can hear it now: "Bring me a solution not a problem." The trouble is that relationships do not lend themselves to the rules of deductive reasoning. All too often I have seen culture change programmes reduced to projects and work packages that introduce new behavioral standards, promote common values and set up new communication systems; yet nothing really changes. It is not that this is wrong, it just is not enough.

So why does the importance of emotions appear to be significantly underplayed in so many businesses? After all, we are often dealing here with very intelligent and highly perceptive individuals. If I argued with them about the power of human emotions they would not challenge me. It is almost a truism. Yet they appear to do so little about it at a systemic organizational level. For me, to unlock this conundrum we must again look to neuroscience.

The problem of the apparent 'denial' of human emotion among business leaders is not that they don't recognize its importance but more that they do not know what to do about it. If they cannot deal with it successfully, it does not appear on their business agenda. Their brain would see it as a threat, not an opportunity, so they have conditioned themselves not to see it or to treat it as something outside everyday business. They are committing no moral crime nor are they guilty of any irrational judgment. Their career life to date has reinforced the importance of rules, systems, compliance, data, authority and personal power. To turn up and suddenly ask organizational leaders to change their ways is one hell of a request, particularly when it appears that nobody else is going to change. When you have survived by the rules of the jungle, letting go of your protective instincts may not seem the wisest move.

So, is there any hope of a more enlightened approach to leading and managing humans in business? Of course there is. You are forgiven if you feel that I have so far painted these faceless business leaders as corporate robots. That is actually very far from the truth. What I am highlighting here are the pressures of the corporate environments we have created. I have never met a business leader who really didn't care about his people. At a close interpersonal level, they know how important the 'people factor' is.

Ultimately, we are all human beings who want to feel good about ourselves and about our relationships with those closest to us. They could not have built their corporate careers without being able to connect with key people along the way. So we have this significant dilemma. Frankenstein has created the monster – the corporate environment, and he wants to start again, but the situation has overtaken him.

Let's go back to the brain. The limbic layer responds to energy via the senses. Written communication alone provides only two-dimensional data: width and height. Depth can only come through energetic transaction, and this means people-contact. Yes, words will trigger associations in our mind but, given that for most people the experience of the corporate environment is one to be viewed with caution, defensive associations are much more likely than positive ones. Most written communication will be greeted with skepticism, as will all normal corporate 'speak', because we have created an environment of conditioned input and response.

The most regular example of this I experience in businesses in the promotion of core organizational values. At some point in these organizations somebody has taken it on themselves to create or promote the organization's values. These values can be seen pictured on walls, in reception, on PowerPoint slides and in the company literature. I am sure the original intentions behind the exercise were good, yet their affect on the actual behavior of the business is minimal. In fact, in many cases the promoted values become the target of increased skepticism as people within the business recognize the gap between the purported values and the reality. You may win compliance in the business environment by rules and structured authorities, but you will not win over relationships by prescriptive behavior. This is the 'hearts and minds' challenge that faces any organization of collective purpose.

More recently, I have noticed a trend towards behavioral descriptors, which are describing the types of behaviors that will demonstrate the desired values. So, for instance, the value may be 'openness' and the behavior may be being approachable. This is undoubtedly a step in the right direction. Values are not something we can see directly in others. All we see and experience is their behavior, so any attempt to match the behavior that best supports the value is welcome. Having said this, there is still a key ingredient missing: feelings. The science demonstrates that ultimately our behavior is driven by our feelings. The real key to sustainable cultural change is therefore to get people to feel differently about the business. Cultural alignment will always be limited without emotional alignment. Simply producing a list of behavioral descriptors will do little more than change the rules of the game – a new set of behavioral guidelines to play to.

So, what can we do about this? To want to be a part of culture change people need to feel safe and feel that the opportunity outweighs the threat. You will remember that this is no easy task. As discussed earlier, the brain is much more geared to sensing threat than it does opportunity. Fear, while a natural protective response, holds us back from changing. It does not have to be fear of anything specific. In fact, uncertainty is the greatest cause of stress, so the simple act of failing to get the message itself across clearly will result in people becoming uncertain. They know something is afoot but they don't understand it. They therefore seek out the refuge of what they already know and hold on to it tighter than ever.

So, while there is much discussion of cultural change within corporate organizations it can only happen if there is change within the individuals who make up the organization. Otherwise, people will stick with their existing internal response mechanisms to deal with the change that is apparently going on around them. They are not part of it and, while they may feel obliged to demonstrate some of the behaviors demanded by the culture change program, they offer only the benefits of superficial compliance.

So how does an organization successfully transform its culture? There are many books written solely on this subject, but I want to keep my argument simple, and I want to do so by sticking to underlying physiological and neuroscientific principles.

First, we have to be able to answer the question why? Why change? Why should anyone take on the risk associated with change without a very good reason? The answer falls into two parts. Part one is to explain why the current rules of survival will not be able to work in the future. In business, this could be a compelling explanation of how the market has moved on and the current product offering is becoming outdated. It could be an operational argument, for example how we need to partner with a new organization to keep our costs down. In my experience, such explanations are usually offered but they are superficial and not enough is done to explain the personal ramifications. Part two is to answer the question as to why the opportunity outweighs the threat. This needs to be energizing. It needs to paint a picture where people can again see themselves not only surviving but thriving. Each person needs to be able to see where they fit into this picture. And this is exactly where the hard work needs to be directed. More typically, the business message is delivered without conviction and with little ability to explain the personal effects. People need to feel the message, not just hear it. Otherwise, feelings will stay in the default setting of sensing threat, and cultural change will be a very difficult challenge.

Second, the essence of culture change is that it must take the form of a sustained *experience*. Having answered the 'Why?' question above, we then have to engage the senses in something real and meaningful. People who feel threatened will not change willingly. They will withdraw into their shells. So, first we have to energize people with the opportunities associated with change. By its very nature, such energizing can only be undertaken on an interpersonal level. This is a vital part of the role of leadership in any organization.

Leadership

> *"A leader is a dealer in hope."*
>
> **—Napoléon Bonaparte (1769-1821)**

Leadership is essentially the skill of getting others to follow. In the business world, to be sustainable means creating a *willing* following. Leaders, whether formally the 'bosses', or informally, the peer-influencers, become the disciples of the change message. If their behavior does not reflect the integrity of the intended change dynamic, people will not follow. Every feature of misaligned leadership behavior will be noticed and will act as another drag on any change momentum. Any instances of putting personal agendas before organizational agendas will ring the death knell of aspiring corporate change.

This runs right to the top of the organization. A fish rots from the head down, so if we don't have it right at the top, the next level of leadership in an organization will always face a major challenge in behaving openly and convincingly with their subordinates. Leaders are people themselves and therefore can only behave in a trustworthy manner if they feel trusted. The rules do not suddenly change as we pass down through the organization.

Client snapshot

Isabelle – steering the right course

People typically seek coaching support when they are facing a personal challenge. It may be a performance issue or a career challenge, but often there is some potential threat to be navigated. On the other hand, occasionally coaching assignments appear that are entirely positive and developmental in nature. This was the case with Isabelle.

Isabelle had been appointed CEO to a major corporate business with a unique business proposition. While a very successful person in her previous roles, some of which carried a significant public profile, she had not performed this type of role before. Her primary style was Think but her Know and Feel were not far behind. This gave her the opportunity to play out a very rounded approach to her leadership of the business.

Her Think style meant that she gave herself time and room to think things through before she committed, which was particularly important in the early stages of getting familiar with a business with so many nuances. It also meant she had an open mind to seeking coaching support. No ego blockages here, just a pragmatic assessment of where her strengths could readily be deployed and where she could benefit from support. Yet her Knowing very quickly gave her a sense of purpose and a belief in where the business should be going. In the early days this was more a personal belief for her to anchor her own thoughts and energy. It was something to be unfolded carefully with trusted colleagues, and she systematically went about adding depth and diligence to her initial instinctive assessment. At the same time, while not typically demonstrative in her behavioral style, she used her Feel capability to sense what was going on around her and to make sound judgments regarding character. She was and is very adept at managing key relationships, able to engage and yet able to maintain appropriate momentum in the pursuit of her sense of purpose.

I am supporting Isabelle in engaging her top team to redefine and rearticulate the long-term strategy for the business. The strategic imperative she faces is fundamental and will challenge many of the existing beliefs and behaviors within the organization. Yet she is setting a tone to the dialog that is challenging but supportive, both assertive in its purpose and flexible in its approach. Fundamental transformation can only come from the top: her people will need to be able to connect with her sense of purpose (Knowing) if they are to willingly accept her leadership. If anyone can do it, Isabelle can.

Unfortunately, we appear to have created corporate organizations where distrust is far too frequently the norm. It may not always be expressed as such; it is more of a default setting: resistance remains underground and is encapsulated not in open conflict but in the safer territory of inertia and apathy. Instead of aligning with the overall organizational culture, which they do not feel a part of, people will align behind the sub-culture that forms the more relevant and enjoyable part of their daily experience, such as their functional team or the people in the office they like to be with. Expecting others to change but not being prepared to change ourselves is the most common source of failure, and any program that does not address this fundamental requirement from the top is doomed to fail.

People respond to the everyday environment of which they are a part, the constant signals and evidence they pick up from those around them. So, if we want a change of behavior, the working environment has to change. Every opportunity has to be taken to reinforce examples of positive behavior and to gradually tempt people out of their naturally defensive ways. They need to feel safe and supported. They need leaders who help them to feel that the business will take them on a journey that is meaningful, relevant and exciting and that will give them the chance to thrive and grow as human beings.

You are forgiven if this now feels like an impossible task. Yet it is the reality. Corporate businesses need a fundamentally different approach to the way they lead and manage the culture of their organizations. This will not be easy, but it is time for leaders of courage to step up to the challenge. Just look at the evidence: where are the organizational role models that can inspire the next generation of talent? They are few indeed. Capitalism itself has become a dirty word. The normal story is of major organizations bereft, with issues of internal mistrust and public disdain. Friction exists between shareholders and executives, and this works its way down through the business. People have so much more to give, but they cannot give it in this environment.

Corporate culture and entrepreneuralism

"Success is the child of audacity."

—Benjamin Disraeli, 1st Earl of Beaconsfield, British prime minister (1804-1881)

I have been very lucky in my coaching experience to have worked with clients from many varied business backgrounds, as well as some outside of business. Broadly my business clients can be categorized as 'corporate' and 'entrepreneurs'.

Typically my work with corporate clients revolves around a strategic approach to people alignment and culture behind a shared vision. Working with entrepreneurs typically involves supporting them to create and fulfill a sustainable business strategy beyond their initial phase of growth.

One of the elusive targets currently pursued in the corporate world is a culture of entrepreneurialism. They believe it will bring a freshness and creativity to their organization. This appears to make sense. Unfortunately, I have yet to see this achieved in what are typically Think-dominated environments. Entrepreneurs work primarily by energy and instincts. They have often chosen their route to success because they could not connect with the more traditional schooling system and business school approach that was primarily learning by study. Entrepreneurs learn by doing and are motivated by the vision of their own success. It is usually the force of their own personalities that creates their initial success. They will then face a very different challenge when it comes to managing increasing scale and having to think more conceptually about the longer-term strategic and structural development of their business.

Client snapshot

Andrew – an extreme case of Knowing

When I first met met Andrew, he was a rising star in a large corporate business. His confident, persuasive manner was clear for all to see; he was larger than life and blessed with a superb intellect. In these early days, he appeared to sweep all before him, and promotion inevitably followed. Returning to the simpler language of the Think, Feel, Know model, Andrew was clearly a primary Knower. He operated very much by his gut instinct and by an intellectual processing power that made him hard to challenge. In fact, he was so impressive as a leader at this early time that his subordinates hardly felt the need to challenge him. His personal gravitas gave him an air of confidence that people found compelling.

However, as Andrew moved up the corporate ladder, things started to change. The talent on which he relied did not desert him, but he found his natural sphere of influence slipping away. Why? In organizational terms, he lost his team. This was not the team that he had initially led: this was a team that had been promoted to lead and this triggered a very different dynamic. There was no basis of loyalty to Andrew in the team. He had to re-establish his credentials from square one, and this was not going to be handed to him on a plate by those he had passed as career competitors. But more interesting than the organizational dynamic is the personal dynamic, by which I mean the way Andrew was choosing to deal with the situation.

His strengths were Know and Think, the ability to be decisive, based on intuition and experience, and the ability to process data and logic at very fast speeds. His behavioral style was very much driven by his cortex and by the basal layer of the brain. These were the bases on which he had built his prior success, but now it wasn't working. What was wrong? He had left behind his Feel abilities, or at least he was no longer using them to good effect. A Knower/ Thinker is often the most challenging sort of person to deal with because he takes a position very quickly and then he backs this up with rational argument. Unfortunately, this use of rationality usually has the primary purpose of supporting the conclusion already reached, which is post-rationalization. It is not that he is necessarily consciously manipulating data. He simply can't see the data any other

153

way. The blinkers are firmly on. The challenge of this style is that it fails to engage people emotionally. Feelers are left behind and without emotional engagement there is no trust, and without trust there is no loyalty.

In his earlier days, Andrew clearly demonstrated his ability to connect with people, so it was not that he was not capable of it. In fact, trust was a major judgment factor in choosing his colleagues and team members. Andrew was not an uncaring man. Indeed he felt certain things very deeply and really wanted to do the right thing. Yet, as his career progressed he relied more and more on snap intuitive judgments about people and situations. The consequence of his impressive Thinking ability was to create an environment of control where his subordinates were subject to strict process compliance requirements and where possession of detail knowledge became a source of power.

In this environment, trust could not flourish. Andrew had missed the opportunity to put the necessary energetic commitment into building relationships with his new colleagues. Ironically, the pace of his progression had laid the foundation for its demise. Eventually, Andrew had created a situation where he was desperately unhappy. He really did care about people but his chosen style had helped to create a position where his vast competences were engaged primarily in personal survival because of the huge pressure he was under. It ultimately became inevitable that he left the business; to stay would have been counterproductive for the business and soul-destroying for him.

From a coaching point of view, the biggest challenge was to get Andrew to recognize that it was himself that needed to change if he wished to succeed in this environment. Every time we met, some genuine promise of progress emerged.

He was a highly self-aware human being when he allowed himself to be, and, of course, the power of coaching is to create the space where people feel sufficiently safe to have a look at themselves. But successful habits of the past die hard. In an organizational environment that had become virtually 'every man for himself' (there were many other things going on in the business that were in no way attributable to him) it is perfectly understandable that Andrew's survival instinct would come to the fore. He got the Feelings part of the equation wrong. His senses had been fine-tuned to problem-setting and confronting threats. The emotions of attachment and trust were left to wither and die, not by design, but because they were too far down the survival list. Without trust there is no loyalty, and without loyalty there is no sustainable leadership.

My hope and belief is that Andrew will take this learning into his next role and put his amazing talents to a more sustainable and enjoyable use.

These respective camps remain largely polarized: they just don't 'get' each other, and they feel that the alternative approach just would not work in their particular environment. And, to a degree they are, of course, correct. Yet, ironically, they have a lot to offer each other, as they understand different sides of the spectrum of business. The corporate leader who understands how to attract and harness entrepreneurial energy and instincts in his business is a very valuable leader; the entrepreneur who can take her business vision beyond her initial instincts and who can truly build on it strategically will inevitably be very rich one day.

Section IV:

Advanced human performance

"Give me a place to stand, and I shall move the world."

—Archimedes of Syracuse (*c.*287 BC-*c.*212 BC)

Ultimate personal performance

"Strength does not come from physical capacity. It comes from an indomitable will."

—Mohandas Gandhi (1869-1948)

Throughout this book, I have used examples of how human behavior and performance can be explained by insights into our neurological makeup, in particular the role of the brain and the heart.

I have explained the principles of Knowing behavior and how Knowing is the point of peak performance, which athletes call being in the 'zone'. The brain receives the external images or creates the internal images that trigger our emotional and behavioral responses. This is our own unique and personal world of neural networks, the structures of neurons and synapses that comprise the associative connectivity of the brain, the complex web of neural pathways that have been created to respond to our immediate environment.

As we move through life, experience results in the laying down of our own personal tapestry of insights, practice and lessons learned. When we have experienced something we will commit this to memory by laying down a neural pathway. The more the experience is repeated the stronger and more rapid the pathway becomes. Myelin (a material made up of protein and fats) encases the pathway and results in the 'hard-wiring' of this response to a given stimulus.

This explains the Knowing response. As the amygdala scans the scene in front of us and spots the association with something familiar, the neural response is activated without any need for cognitive processing: we don't need to think about it, we just do it – and we expect to succeed. It is this expectation of success that creates confident performance. In this way, professional sportspeople practice incessantly to refine their skills. In this sense, skill is the set of refined execution instructions that deliver the optimal motor-neural response. Practice makes perfect. Or does it?

Well, if this was all that was involved, success would be entirely predictable: it would be just a matter of replaying all the same internal instructions and execution responses that led to success in practice. But it isn't that simple. Any athlete in any sport knows that there is so much more involved when it comes to the heat of battle. So, what is different?

Well, of course, those annoying opponents pop up again. They just will not stick to the script, will they? More importantly, the key difference is the intensification of emotion. Unlike the privacy and safety of the practice ground, we are plunged into the arena of public exposure. The aspirations of glory that motivated us to train and prepare are now combined with the fear of disappointment and failure. Feelings motivate us to follow the journey, but they do not help us in the moment of performance. We will not open the door to Knowing performance without going through Feeling first, yet once it is opened, we need to close the door behind us on feelings if we are to be truly in the zone.

Client snapshot

Hugh – soul-searching

Hugh was an entrepreneur and a very strong Knower. He had worked his way up from the shop floor and was now the main shareholder of a medium-sized business. He was a tough, no-nonsense character with a very energetic and engaging style (secondary Feel). The people he started with in business were still his friends and fellow shareholders. They had deeply loyal relationships. However, Hugh's business had probably gone as far as it could with the existing team. Hugh himself was ready for, and capable of, dealing with bigger things, but he knew his team members and friends would struggle to take this extra step. So he had a real battle of conscience in allowing himself to move on.

Hugh's deep sense of values was potentially in conflict here – his sense of loyalty battling with his drive for further business and personal growth. Ultimately, it was his sense of Knowing that got him through this. A Feeler would have struggled to make the breakthrough. When it came to the crunch, he showed the same resilience that he had needed in order to be successful in business in the first place. Yet he did not have to compromise his sense of personal loyalty to achieve this. He worked out a plan that gave his colleagues every chance to extend their role and their shareholding in his current business, and he made sure they were supported in their attempts to achieve this. Hugh himself then went on to buy another bigger business.

I have explained that Knowing is a very selfish place, but the word 'selfish' is too judgmental. It does not mean that we do not care about others, which comes through Feel. In Knowing, we find comfort in ourselves and the Knowing of who we are and what really drives us. Even though we may not easily be able to articulate this, we just know it: it comes from the gut. When we understand what drives us we need to respond to it: to do otherwise creates inner conflict and nobody has the right to expect us to be something we are not. We can only give our most by being who we are. Hugh did his soul-searching and found his answers.

Ultimate personal performance is about feelings v focus. In the moment, feelings will distract us, so we have to find ways of maintaining our focus despite all the emotional distractions that surround us. Does this mean we have to become robots? Actually, while there are some parallels, the answer is no. Being robotic means closing down many of our natural sensing mechanisms that will be vital to responding to our environment at the time of ultimate performance demand. So, the real task here is to close down the unhelpful emotional responses but, somehow, we need to keep our senses open and alert to our immediate surroundings. Sounds tough? Of course it is tough: that is why so few among us achieve it. And yet, by understanding the principles, this level of performance need not be as elusive as it seems. So, how do athletes and, indeed, successful people in general, achieve this?

Let's take the athlete first. I don't need to go through their whole training regime here. It should be established by now that dedication to practicing the chosen art is an absolute prerequisite to sustained success. Likewise, the successful businessperson will need to dedicate a significant part of her life to learning the rules and then fine-tuning her execution if she is to build a sustainable career. But how do we control our emotions? I start from the place of saying that emotions cannot be 'controlled'. For me, this conjures up images of repressing natural feelings, of denial and inner conflict. Feelings cannot be switched off or brushed under the carpet; they need to be acknowledged and worked through. The real key to ultimate performance is that the emotional conflict should not be there in the first place. Essentially, we have to be at peace with the cause that is driving us.

When the techniques of our trade are truly understood and their execution mastered to a high level of finely tuned certainty, all that remains is for us to believe in what we are doing. When we put this belief into practice we are experiencing who we want to be. Life is giving us the feedback to reinforce our belief in who we are, and the journey becomes self-fulfilling. And the deeper our conviction of who we really are the more sustainable the performance becomes. This is the ultimate; we are being who we really are. No energy is wasted; everything is committed to the cause. No emotional distress, no distraction, just a flowing performance that takes us to another plane. Watch athletes in the zone, watch classical musicians lost in their music, watch the people who truly believe.

Personal change

"The real voyage of discovery consists not in seeking new landscapes, but in having new eyes."

—Marcel Proust, French novelist, critic, and essayist (1871-1922)

Can people really change? There are many conversations about this, and opinion seems to be fairly mixed. I feel it is useful to look at this from a neuroscientific perspective. There is no clear answer to the specific question posed, but we can improve our understanding of the dynamics.

Here it is important to recall the earlier explanation of the way we build up our view of ourselves through life. We start laying down the early years of experience through emotional memories and recollections. Slowly, primarily through the development of the pre-frontal cortex, we learn to reflect and make sense of these experiences, and from this interaction of experience and reflection emerges our view of ourselves. As we go through adolescence the need for a sense of personal identity strengthens with every hormonal step. We are no longer content just to be a reflection of our parents. We deserve recognition in our own right. So the story of our chosen life's journey starts to unfold. Yet, in life terms, we still have so much to learn.

Along the way, we will be confronted with key decision points and defining moments. In the search for certainty, we will constantly look for evidence of reinforcement of our choices. For some these choices will be easy while for others they will be difficult. Our brains will always seek comfort in familiarity, so we typically build our own walls of resistance to change. Any challenge to this state of certainty will be met initially with skepticism, especially as we get older and the lessons of life become more deeply sewn into our psyche.

Yet, this cannot be the full story. The most fundamental genetic drive sitting at the deepest part of our heritage is the desire not only to survive but also to thrive. Why else would species evolve to keep pace with their environmental demands? Thriving is not achievable without some change and some risk. Genetically, we understand that staying stagnant is not an option. So resistance to change is the natural first intuitive survival barrier we all present, albeit to differing degrees, when confronted with something we do not understand. Yet, at a deeper level we also feel the need to look for opportunities to thrive. This is the gateway to personal change.

Most lives consist of choices made, consciously or otherwise, and consequences experienced. In general, we are programmed to look for the familiar. Yet occasionally something or someone will happen to us that makes us reconsider our own design for life. Sometimes such interventions are sought by us as we feel our sense of purpose and enjoyment slipping away, and sometimes we remain in denial about our desire and need to change, until life comes along and changes the rules for us.

There are many testimonies in the public domain from people who have experienced life-changing moments through deep personal experiences, such as life-threatening illnesses or incidents. Somehow, in these moments, people can discover a propensity to change that they never previously believed was possible. Their whole life meaning has changed because they have experienced something new at an intense, emotional level. Their previous perspective is rendered useless because the boundaries of their existence have been extended. Yet such testimonies are communicated with an intriguing sense of calm. Moments of personal change are not moments of high anxiety or excitement; these factors have undoubtedly contributed to the feeling of the need to change but not the decision itself. It is as though when we really know what change has to be made we drop to a deeper level of our existence and engage with a new depth of meaning. The decision to change and the path we then choose is taken calmly and decisively. Once made, there is no going back. Our lives will never be the same again.

But what of less extreme change, such as the change of behavior required to enhance career prospects or the cultural changes sought by business organizations? The principles are the same: the only difference is the gravity of the change. Crucially, the brain has to perceive an opportunity that outweighs the threat. And this is no easy task. Remember here we are not talking about the logical weighing up of pros and cons and sequential processing leading up to a rational conclusion. We are talking about emotions. Logic only gets a chance if emotions allow it. Each of us has built up our own emotional crutch based on our personal life experience. Then someone comes along and asks us to throw the crutch away. On the other hand, we will never learn to run if we continue to hold on to the crutch. Logically, and even visually, the argument could be persuasive, but there is no way we will let that crutch go unless we are convinced we will not fall over.

So the process of supporting personal change is first and foremost an emotional transaction that allows the client to work out for herself that the opportunities outweigh the threats. When the client is appropriately emotionally engaged to take on the challenge, the next steps are all about what needs to be done and how, which are the techniques of effecting personal change.

Client snapshot

John – learning to take some risks

John worked for a nationally recognized charity. He was a naturally caring man who had always worked in social services or not-for-profit organizations. His career had been reasonably successful, getting to the higher end of middle management, but that next step had eluded him. Despite many attempts he had not been offered the opportunity to move to the next level. John had a very strong Think profile and while his deliberate approach and careful communication style had assisted his career to date, it was now hampering him. It is not that the Think style itself is a weakness, but an overdependence on any one style certainly is, and here was an example of a strength overplayed becoming a weakness.

John's problem was that he offered minimal energy in his style. His tonality was very flat and his mannerisms ponderous. There was no doubting his intellect, but most people do not connect with intellect alone. He was now aspiring to bigger leadership roles, and his perceived inability to energize was seen as a major inhibition. In parallel, his tendency to over-process and over-complicate meant that he was slow to get to the point, again an unacceptable trait for a leader. Leadership is about impact and direction. He openly admitted that he felt the need to examine questions from all angles before committing to an answer. To cap it all, the fact that he was such a nice guy meant that colleagues and advisers had rarely been direct in their feedback on these issues. They would "dance around the houses" (John's words) and, although well intentioned, this was not helping him move forward.

So the coaching conversation with John was focused on supporting him to change his behavior. The cause for optimism with John is that he is very honest. When it got to the point that he asked for very direct feedback from me, that's exactly what he got. Some of my language was very challenging, but John and I had built up sufficient trust for him to know that I was trying to help him. He was shocked at first. Although nothing that I said really surprised him, hearing it without any 'dressing-up' knocked him back. Of course, as a coach, I did not make this judgment lightly, but John was so trapped in conditioned behavior that was holding him back that we both agreed it was worth the risk. In true Think style, he needed time to process what I had said, so we left further dialog to our next monthly session. And true enough, he came bouncing back the next time, truly grateful for the feedback and determined to start doing something about it.

People trapped in conditioned behavior can only move forward by experimenting with new behaviors. Turning up for work and trying to behave like somebody you are not will not work, though; authenticity will always be a key element of real connection with others. I would therefore encourage John, as an example, to bounce into the office some mornings with a smile on his face. I would press him for quick intuitive answers without allowing him processing time, something he found incredibly difficult. We only develop new skills by practicing them (ideally in safe environments), and we only get feedback on these behavioral experiments and modifications by putting them out there. The barrier to doing so is usually ourselves, not the people we are dealing with. And as we get feedback on what we are trying to do, so we are able to navigate our way to a more productive style without having to sacrifice our authenticity. More than that, learning about yourself in this way can actually be enlightening and enjoyable.

Most frequently as a coach I am asked to support people who operate at senior levels in business. For them, the challenge is not about learning another management theory: they have been there and worn the T-shirt many times. Their challenges are not logical; they are intensely personal and subjective. For many who are well into their (successful) careers the flames of ego fulfillment and public success no longer burn brightly enough to give them access to the source of self-generating energy they need to perform their demanding roles. All that glittered was not gold and, while their original passion undoubtedly served them well in getting them to where they are now, ironically where they are now is not such a great place to be, after all.

Clients in this energetic space are usually facing the challenge of personal reinvention. This does not mean throwing away all the energy sources in their lives that still work for them. But it does mean having the courage to recognize that they have moved on as human beings and that hanging on to those things that energized them in the past but no longer have the same effect, is a form of evolutionary stagnation. At our deepest genetic level we know this is not a sustainable option.

The coaching and support of human change is therefore a process of understanding what the crutches are in our lives, which ones still have a useful role to play and which are just getting in the way of progress. For those who have disconnected from their previous sources of motivation, it becomes a case of understanding what is really important to them now. What does the person they are now really connect with? It is enormously rewarding to see people reconnect with their sense of purpose, to see the light of inspiration begin to reappear in their faces. It is a tragic irony that so many powerful people appear to feel that acknowledging the need for personal change represents a weakness – an admission that we have got something wrong in the past, that...wait for it...we weren't perfect after all. Yet, it is exactly this acknowledgment about what we need to leave behind that creates the energetic space where we can regenerate the energy we need to continue to thrive. A battery cannot be successfully recharged if it is still full of 'dirty' energy.

And these principles stand up whether we are considering personal change for the individual or if we are looking at whole-scale cultural change across a large group of people. To update the classic axiom, engage the brains and the hearts – and the bodies will follow.

Physiological intervention

"Until you stop breathing, there's more right with you than wrong with you."

—Jon Kabat-Zinn, professor of medicine emeritus, University of Massachusetts Medical School (1944-)

Many of my clients and colleagues have asked me about techniques for controlling anxiety and stress or enhancing wellbeing. This is not directly the purpose of this book, but I am happy to touch on this briefly here, as it again confirms the physiological and neurological principles I am exploring and is certainly relevant to understanding confident performance.

There are many techniques in use for psychological intervention in human behavior and probably an even wider selection of physiological interventions. People and professions are in a constant search for antidotes to stress and anxiety. Here I want to focus on the basic principles that should underpin any physiological intervention aimed at inducing a state of calm or feeling of positivity. Within this, I will explain broadly what happens within our bodies to bring about the desired results.

Let's look first at the ways in which we typically try to control our own behavior. Social conformity demands that we do not react entirely intuitively, emotionally or without regard for our affect on others. Unfettered behavioral responses would be very interesting but not always socially productive. I would suggest that there are typically three levels of personal intervention in our own responses and behavior patterns.

The most common is behavioral control. This means that we are trying to constrain ourselves to a deliberate, preconsidered behavioral response, sometimes described as 'keeping your grip'. Curiously, like so many of these phrases, it is very apt as it implies keeping a grip (or lid) on our emotions. At this level, emotions are something to be kept in the private space of our own bodies rather than matters for public display. And, of course, without some compliance with these rules, society could not function.

When we are 'controlling' minor or even moderate emotions this can be done easily and without any unnecessary bodily trauma. Yet, when the anxiety stakes rise, the more difficult the task becomes, the cracks in our social mask begin to appear. More importantly, we are internalizing powerful emotions: emotions are energy and energy cannot be destroyed, so the anxiety continues to bounce around the body, either openly or apparently hidden away, only to be resurrected every time there is a memory association that is triggered. So, behavior control, while socially essential, can also be the source of health decline. I am sure we all know people who have bottled up their emotions until any intervention was too late.

The problem with this type of intervention is that it is triggered only at the very end of the behavioral response cycle. The emotional and health damage may already be done. So we have to examine ways of intervening in our responses earlier.

If we want to get ahead in the emotional response game, the first thing we can do is get to understand and spot the triggers. Each of us will have built through life our programmed responses to those situations or people that attract us, threaten us, or sadden us. It can be very productive to be clear about what exactly these triggers are.

When it comes to negative triggers, we usually find it difficult to analyze them rationally because of the associative emotion attached to the experience. Yet, there is value to be gained in reflection here, when the intensity of the pain has died down, to try to spot patterns in our defensive responses. No doubt, many of these conditioned responses are well founded and appropriate to maintain, but some may be irrational, currently irrelevant and putting us through needless anxiety.

As we spot these unnecessary instances and patterns, we need to rewrite the rules in the brain. The rules we have already laid down are no longer serving us and need to be removed or rewritten. If they are deeply ingrained this may not be easy to achieve, but there will be others that are not so deep but are just as inhibiting. They need to be rationally flushed out. The more you explain to yourself rationally that your conditioned response to these triggers is no longer necessary, the more you will convince your brain that it is OK to drop its guard in relation to this particular issue. The rule was only ever written to protect you, so don't get angry with yourself, just get yourself updated.

It is then a matter of getting ahead of the game emotionally by spotting the triggers as soon as they come on to your personal radar. This may seem like a contradiction since, as I explained earlier in the book, this is exactly what the amygdala does: the difference here is that you are looking for the trigger and have the rewritten response (the rational case for dismissing the threat) ready to hand. The brain will gradually learn to access the new 'solution' and the risk of threat response is reduced. You are training the brain to turn a previously held fear response into a rational and currently appropriate reaction.

So, spotting the likely triggers to our emotional responses will give us the first defence against unhelpful reactions, yet there is no way that such a defence can be impregnable. There will always be those threats that will penetrate regardless of any radar or defensive wall. They are too powerful and sometimes dangerously camouflaged in the appearance of everyday events. Then what else can we do? This brings us to the area of emotional resilience. By mastering appropriate psycho-physiological techniques we can build our emotional resilience to such a level that even the most challenging of threats can be rebuffed without harm to health or performance. This sounds a bit grand and too good to be true, so we need to have a closer look.

There are a range of techniques available that broadly follow the principles outlined in the example I describe here. I am not recommending just one approach, but I want to explain what the key elements are to sustaining a significant benefit. This example is for personal use, and there are similar examples that can be applied to the sporting arena.

This exercise involves getting settled comfortably in a chair that adequately supports both your back and your legs. It is important to choose an environment that is quiet and where you will feel at ease. The next step is to concentrate on your breathing. This is a key step as it is a way of bypassing the brain, where we may be experiencing all sorts of confusion and clutter. This approach takes us via the lungs directly to the heart. As we become more attuned to our breathing our minds will gradually relax, and our hearts will take over. The cortex and limbic layers can ease down, as there is no imminent threat, and the response of the body is largely autonomic, requiring no new instructions. We need to continue with this focus on breathing for a few minutes. To gain the most physiological benefit it is important to keep the breathing constant and reasonably robust. It is not so much deep breathing as active breathing, say about five seconds in and seven seconds out: this should actively exercise the heart without causing undue strain. You should not continue if you feel any discomfort.

Having accessed the first level of relaxation, the second step is to introduce a positive personal experience into the exercise. This is done by remembering or imagining a special event in our lives when we felt loved and valued and experienced a deep sense of peace, or a special person who made us feel that way. For those more spiritually inclined, this could be a higher presence. At this point we are supporting the brain to access positive internal references. Fundamentally, we feel good, and the better we get at doing this, the deeper the sense of wellbeing. This is the essence of meditation. At first, it will not be easy to hold on to the emotional experience, as we are conditioned to having lively minds that are easily distracted. However, we shouldn't get angry or frustrated. We just need to lead our attention back to where we want it to be.

We should try to sustain this experience for approximately 10 minutes. Enjoy the scene and relax into the sense of peace. We should imagine ourselves as the actor in the scene, not the director. This is not something we are spectating; it is an experience. We have to imagine ourselves being there and personally immersed in the situation: the camera is our eyes and the feelings are our own. The scene may be one of a grassy clearing in a wood on a summer's day where you encounter someone very special from your life; it may be surveying the horizon as the sea gently flows up and around your feet. You should access the scene that gives you the greatest sense of peace, all the time maintaining the steady flow of breathing that will continue to calm your body. As you move towards the end of this exercise, you can gently let the scene go, continue your breathing pattern for a minute or so longer and then slowly regain your awareness of what is going on around you.

Typically, the total exercise needs to last for about 15 minutes if it is to induce the desired hormonal balance changes. The effect of this intervention should be to release more DHEA into the body and to reduce cortisol. For sustainable health benefit, the exercise needs to be repeated three times a week.

Having followed a regime like this myself for some time, I can testify that the benefits are very tangible. For me, apart from the direct relaxation enjoyed in the exercise itself and the general sense of enhanced wellbeing, within weeks of starting I could feel my heart and lungs getting stronger. I suffered bronchitis as a child, so my lungs were not always as strong as they might have been, but every medical or ECG I have taken since undertaking this exercise regime has shown strong performance on all counts. This is no coincidence.

And do not underestimate the potential here in terms of power and clarity of thought. As you relax into this regime, your thoughts can slowly become disentangled and, with practice, you will allow room for fresh light and insight.

The classic example here is Buddhist monks. Until recent times, these monks had been inaccessible to science, but the Dalai Lama changed this. The strength of his belief means that he is not threatened by scientific exploration, and so he has been happy for his monks to work with scientists in areas such as the development of the mind. His approach is that he has his beliefs, and these will remain unless something comes along to show him that he is mistaken. This wonderful state of openness has led to a level of collaboration between religion and science that is quite inspiring.

The relevance here is that Buddhist monks have subjected themselves to laboratory research to understand the power and functioning of their minds. They are important subjects because of the time and dedication they have devoted to meditation, which is effectively an extension and intensification of the exercise described above. These monks can spend up to seven hours per day meditating on the state of their humanity and spirituality. When it comes to visualization and focus these guys are well ahead of the field. Their laboratory results provided conclusive evidence of this. Not only were they able to sustain concentration for periods well beyond the norm, but the strength and consistency of the electrical output from their hearts throughout the experiments was also remarkable, showing physiological evidence of extreme cardiac health and profound emotional stability.

You only have to meet a Buddhist monk to see the informal evidence for yourself: the immediate impact of their natural grace and warmth and their smiling, reassuring faces is a pleasure to behold. The monks themselves describe the meditation experience as looking out over a calm ocean on a beautiful day. Some thoughts may pass like birds flying across the horizon and quickly disappear, but they will not disturb the calm of the ocean or the ultimate feeling of peace.

Back in our western world of hustle and bustle, these mediation-like experiences can give us a glimpse of the ocean. And remarkably, insights can appear in the calmness of our mind. Here we are slowing down the cortex and supporting it to relax from making rational sense of our everyday experiences. Our limbic layer is completely at ease, as there is no sense of threat: we are therefore in an ideal position to get back in touch with ourselves at the deepest level. Normally access to the basal layer is triggered by our everyday scanning and matching mechanisms; but now we are exploring ourselves, not in response to any particular external trigger but just because it is the place where we go when we feel at peace. Now the whole world of our life data is available to us and powerful insights and answers can come to us without being asked.

Bringing this back to sporting performance is also relevant here. As discussed earlier, regimes for developing confidence in top level athletes are now common place, virtually a prerequisite to top level competitive success. The principle is the same: confidence is the mind and body feeling at peace with their ability to perform a given task. For the athlete, the positive scene is the sporting challenge – the visualization of successfully completing the task ahead. The athlete must learn to love his mind, his body and his challenge if he is to perform to his ultimate ability.

In a western world dominated by the call for determination, focus, diligence and resilience, I find it intriguing that truly ultimate performance depends more on factors such as love and peace.

Section V:

Organizational physiology

"Snowflakes are one of nature's most fragile things, but just look what they can do when they stick together."

—Vista M. Kelly

A scenario for organizational design and development

Earlier in the book, I expressed my own views and frustrations about the corporate organizational environment that we have built. This is based on many years of being a part of such organizations and on my experiences as a coach. It is understandable that competitive organizations should sometimes suffer performance-related stress, but the systematic exposure to pressure and judgment that many corporate employees have to face is totally unreasonable, immoral and ultimately counterproductive. The evidence is commonplace. Most corporate organizations are fighting with challenges of low morale. Some may put this down to the lengthy recession experienced by most western businesses. Yet, these same organizations also fear the economic upturn in the sense that they will then battle with an inability to retain their employees. Many people are just waiting for the chance to find a new employer and will vote with their feet when the opportunities reappear.

It is all too easy just to blame those at the top. The average length of tenure of CEOs of corporate organizations has been consistently reducing over recent decades as the demand for immediate results intensifies. The pressure that some organizational leaders face is ridiculous. The approach sometimes seems to be – when things aren't going to plan, get a new CEO in, flog him or her for as long as he or she can take it, then get rid and bring in the next candidate for flogging. Shareholders are not free from blame: the constant pursuit of short-term profit and value-growth is a key contributor to modern corporate life. All of this leaves me with this deep sense of missed opportunity. People are capable of giving so much more than these environments allow.

Thus, I want to present the seeds of an alternative to the current approach. Of course, a debate about organizational design and development could fill another book but what I really want to achieve here is provoking the right conversations. In general, too many business organizations are avoiding the conversation. They will explore fully how the current modus operandi can be improved, but little is done to explore a radically different approach. Why? Partly because of vested interests: those who currently hold power probably feel that they would be putting this power at risk if they changed the rules. After all, for all the shortcomings of this organizational environment, these guys have demonstrated that they know how to play the corporate game of career success. It feels too much like turkeys voting for Christmas. Or is it simply that they don't know how to change this culture? Where there is uncertainty there is fear.

In an attempt to start addressing this, I will not present a prescriptive blueprint for organizational design. It is unlikely that a one-size-fits-all approach will suffice here. The subject matter is too complex and too deeply ingrained. I will, however, present some principles that, I believe, could underpin organizational performance and development in the future.

The root cause of the problem is that most modern business organizations have evolved from Taylorism, the dominant 'scientific management' approach that emerged from the Industrial Revolution (its development began with Frederick Winslow Taylor in the 1880s and 1890s within the manufacturing industries). Taylorism treats people as working units, breaking everything human down to the lowest common denominator, stripping human potential down to the predictability of factory machines. By reducing all activities to the most basic level, they could become measurable and therefore manageable. Emotions were not predictable, and so were rendered irrelevant in the workplace. There was no room for trust; this could not be captured in a time and motion study. In fact, the whole premise underpinning this management style was that of mistrust. Workers could not be trusted to be committed to their work through human willingness, so the work operation was designed to counter human motivational risk.

Of course, today's work environment is not this bad: we rarely have to face the atrocious physical demands of the early factories and mines. However, there are still unhealthy hangovers. There is still the preoccupation with processes and procedures, authority structures, job descriptions and measurable evidence. It is not that these have no place in such organizations; without them we would see chaos, just like the sports team that has no plan. Yet there is a major issue of balance. As we generally have not really understood how to manage human potential and culture, it is left to the chance of occasional enlightenment from the minority: meanwhile the machine of structured human processing continues to thrive.

Humans are not revenue- or cost-generating units. If you did not already know, I hope the principles explained in this book have helped you to acknowledge and feel secure in the fact that we are fundamentally emotional beings. For me, it is a complete contradiction that corporate organizations shy away from this absolute fact, typically seeking comfort in the strictly logical and very familiar world of structure and data. Emotions are energy and cannot be destroyed, but they are driven underground, like any form of prohibition. We have created an organizational black market for trading on emotions and this opens up the opportunity for abuse. We have created too many organizations that are built on fear, and where there is fear there are bullies.

So, my intention here is to offer some design and development principles that have the potential to take organizations beyond the overtly Think-dominated environment that is currently serving us so poorly. My premise is that organizations of the future need to be based on physiological principles. To date, we have built organizations that reflect machines, and our humanity has been lost along the way. Now that neuroscience is able to give us the comfort of compelling evidence of what really drives us and our responses, we have the opportunity to design organizations as living organisms that truly reflect what and who we really are. Surely, if we create an environment that closely reflects our own natural dynamics, we are most likely to be at one with, and therefore in flow with, the community of which we are a part. Future organizations should not be viewed as authority structures where everything revolves around power. The next organizational generation needs to set out to create motivated communities with a shared business purpose. Those who achieve this first will reap the rewards deserved by their insight and courage.

So, how might this next organizational generation look? My proposition is that future organizations need to be designed on balanced Think, Feel and Know principles. For me, part of the weakness of current organizational thinking is that these three elements are thrown together into one melting pot, with Think inevitably rising to the surface and Feel being consigned to the underworld. In future, the principles and accountabilities underpinning each have to be clearly differentiated. Fundamentally, there should be three parts of the business:

The Think element of the organization – responsible for **information**.

The Feel element – responsible for the **people** in the business.

The Know element – responsible for **decisions** and **direction**.

All three elements will play a vital role, and ultimately it is the interaction between these areas that will determine the level of success.

The Feel Organization

"What the heart knows today, the head will understand tomorrow."

—James Stephens, Irish poet and storyteller (1882-1950)

I will start with the Feel principle because it is the least familiar and, for some, will be the most radical. Those responsible for the Feel area of an organization need to be clearly and separately identified. Feel here means direct responsibility for the people that comprise the business. They are responsible for the people who are the 'factory' of the organization, the people who deliver product and service, who sell and distribute. These are the real people leaders in the business, and they should be responsible for the development and alignment of human value and potential. They need to be interpersonally skilled and naturally in tune with people energy and culture; indeed, they are responsible for its guardianship and development.

In today's business environment typically there is the occasional HR specialist to advise on culture. This proposal aims to flip this and make this responsibility central to the whole organization and distributed to where it really belongs – at the coalface of the operation. While there is undoubtedly a major requirement for clarity and skill-development, human performance is driven largely by the way we feel about ourselves, our environment, the challenge in front of us and the people we work with. The Feel leaders in the business are responsible for getting the best out of their people, and they will do this by their ongoing ability to inspire, support, mentor and coach.

Crucially, they are not directly responsible for the business tasks that have to be performed in the business. These will be owned by the Think organization. In this way, the Feel leaders can be freed up to support and develop their people. Their accountability to the Think element of the organization is to provide the people, energy and motivation to get the job done, but not to define the job. This is vital to ensuring that the right amount of attention is given to developing the people value of the organization.

Today, it is largely left to managers to balance people requirements with the more measurable outputs of business performance. The problem is that in a measures-dominated environment, there are no pressing figures to be reported on people value and motivation. They do not appear directly on either the profit and loss account or the balance sheet. What do appear are sales, costs, profit and cash, and it is these factors that drive managerial behavior. Ultimately, organizations get what they deserve and, if the 'bottom-line' is profit, everything will evolve around this. The contradiction is that all these financial measures are indirect evidence of one primary source, which is people endeavor. What the profit and loss account does not report is missed possibilities. Financial measures are inevitably historic and do not report on what is going on in the organization now.

Attempts have been made over the last decade to develop the credentials of human capital management, that is the discipline that attempts to define business measures that capture the value of people in an organization. Maybe there is something in this in the long term, but for now I believe that our energy is much better spent simply acknowledging that people value cannot be measured in classic business terms. We all know how important the 'people factor' is, so instead of reverting to our normal conditioned behavior of reducing everything to Think measures, let's just get on with developing the energy source of our business. We will know when it is working because we will feel it, and this will be reflected in the health of the business and in all the traditional financial measures that will monitor this.

The technology industry is an example of a business sector that has touched on some of the principles by creating common pools of people talent who are then placed in projects as the need arises. This has been driven more by principles of efficiency than by a real understanding of energy. General commentary from those I have talked to about this type of organizational arrangement suggests that this was usually difficult, mainly because project owners wanted direct control of their own resources. After all, if their heads as project managers were first 'on the chopping block' they did not want to chance their fate to colleagues with different accountabilities. This form of matrix management, like all the others, presents real challenges in managing the distribution of power and the relationships that should negotiate this.

My view is that such design rules do not go far enough. Usually the balance of power is tilted in favor of the project managers and the 'resource owners' in the business are relegated to levels of housekeeping. Again the short-term demands of the business are allowed to take over. Alternatively, the balance could favor the resource owners and impenetrable fiefdoms would result. My proposition is that equal perceived value and authority needs to be devolved so that project managers and people leaders have to work closely and equally to reach performance targets, both short and longer term. This needs to be supported by a culture that values collaboration and teamwork and challenges territorialism and authority abuse.

The role of the people leader then is to develop the competence, wellbeing and performance potential of her team of people. Project or task managers in the business need to be seen as internal customers whose needs have to be met wherever possible. The people leaders will ensure they deliver the competence and energy necessary to get the job done.

Even my explanation of this is weak because it is structural, as I suspect that this is where the practical debate would start in many organizations. However, the power of the change rests in the effect it will have energetically. Please recall at this point the functioning of the brain and the heart and how we are driven first by scanning for any threat to our survival. If we continue to perceive personal threat in our working environment, much of our energy will be directed towards sophisticated games of personal survival. In organizations that struggle to acknowledge us for who we really are, there will always be a perceived threat, sometimes an explicit one, sometimes one existing as an implicit undercurrent.

To change this, people have to feel attracted to an opportunity that outweighs any sense of threat. When the amygdala gives the OK, the brain knows what to do, we feel good about the challenge in front of us and we can step up to a new level of performance. The people leaders, if appropriately skilled and supported, will transform the culture and the people. They will understand the power of the culture that people experience every day and constantly commit themselves to enriching this experience. Strategically, they will be invaluable, as they will have the potential to align the total energy of the business behind one vision and one purpose. This is the road to true advanced collective human performance, a world we can only glimpse today.

The Think Organization

"It is the province of knowledge to speak and it is the privilege of wisdom to listen."

—Oliver Wendell Holmes, American lecturer and author (1809-1894)

So, while the Feel leaders are responsible for the development of people value, the Think element of the organization is responsible for information value. The key consideration here is that this is information presented and maintained without emotion. It is about clarity and objectivity unedited by personal or political agendas. It will typically fall into a number of areas.

First, there is the traditional *reporting* data that every business needs in order to monitor its operations. This will always include financial data and will probably include other operational performance measures. This is the domain of the specialist, the knowledge experts who truly understand their fields. Financial specialists are an obvious example.

Second, there is the information that defines the *requirements* of the business. This could be far ranging, including product and project specifications, client requirements, legal constraints and environmental considerations. The purpose of this information is to channel the energy of the people of the business into targeted business outcomes. This will include both customer and internal projects. Appropriate experts would need to be defined in each area to create and maintain the value of this information.

Third, there will be the *process* information that defines the way in which human activities are planned to create specific outcomes. This is all about best practice and repeatable behavior, the plan by which the business operates. The key value here is scalability. Without this, we will be constantly and unnecessarily reinventing the wheel.

Fourth, there will be the *technical* or *product* knowledge base: the understanding of the technicalities of the business operation, as well as the potential for development, and making this information available to the wider organization. Often this would be seen as the domain of the chief technology officer (CTO) or equivalent.

Fifth, there will be general *awareness* information, which does not need to be distilled to the level of specific tasks, but which is a necessary part of us keeping in touch with our external environment. Marketing communications would fit into this area.

Sixth, there is the *energetic* and *people* data that will emerge over time and will help us to objectively develop the human value of the business: currently virgin territory.

The list above is illustrative and not exhaustive. The key point is recognizing that responsibility for reporting data should sit outside those emotionally attached to the data. The cultural piece for the whole organization here is critical in terms of extending the feeling that objective data is there to be shared in order to add to the value of the business. It is not there to flood the business in detail and is not to be used to batter people into submission and compliance.

The Know Organization

"A good head and a good heart are always a formidable combination."

—Nelson Mandela (1918-)

This leaves the Knowing element of the organization. This is the place where critical decisions are made and the direction of the business is set. It is the place where the Think and Feel parts of the organization are brought together to support the total alignment and operation of the business. It is therefore necessarily the domain of the CEO or the head of the business. Yet, it also goes much deeper than this.

This is the place where the DNA of the organization is laid down. In terms of the brain, it is the place where we draw not only on the lessons of our own experiences, but also those of our predecessors. Here we operate intuitively but also balance this with the factual and energetic data available to us. The brain knows when to call the shots directly, but it also accepts that there are times when the heart is better placed to lead the body. Likewise, the outlook of this CEO will be all about harnessing the total potential of the organization within the context of the chosen direction for the business and the data and energy available within it.

This may look like an approach that would take decision-making power to the top, rendering the rest of the organization powerless. This is not the intention. The DNA of the natural organism runs throughout the body. It is deeply embedded right down to the individual cellular structure. The natural state of our bodies is for the brain and heart to oversee the running of a balanced organism, only directly engaging in exceptional interventions when it has to. Hence we have the distribution of neurological scripts that allow the various parts of the body to get on with their job without undue dependence on the brain. In the same way, the DNA ('Decision Natural Authority'?) of the business needs to be cascaded to a level that befits the natural competences of the areas concerned.

The key consideration is that decisions can only be devolved with due recognition of the balanced consideration of factual and energetic information. One side cannot have the final say over the other. Our brains understand this. If our Think and Feel dynamics are not aligned we are not ready to make a quality decision: we are out of balance. We can only access Knowing when these factors are aligned. The truth is that many day-to-day decisions can be made without anxiety of conflict if they sit within the normal scope of the experience of those making the decisions. Decisions based on poor alignment, such as those made simply because we feel the need to make them, run a high risk of turning out to be poor decisions.

So, on the one hand, decision-making authority needs to be actively devolved to as low a level as competence and information availability will allow. On the other hand, there should be no shame in referring upwards for decision-making support if the wider experience base of the CEO or top team could prove crucial. In this way, this aspect of the Knowing role of the CEO's office is systemic, that is, ensuring that decision-making authority and competence are effectively devolved and calibrated across the organization.

I admit to having another and more challenging agenda here. My proposition is, over time, to take away authority from those who aim to keep it for themselves. This is a key aspect of changing the current paradigm of management behavior. As I stated earlier, we have built corporate organizations in no small part on mistrust and fear. This triggers the survival instinct of those who seek to prosper in these environments. People cannot be blamed for this: in fact, it is a natural law of evolution that the most adaptable survive. The problem here is that this adaptability to date has been largely about the acquisition of power. It is hardly surprising then that the corporate world has inadvertently perpetuated and promoted a gladiatorial arena of personal power and a feeling of 'every man for himself'. If this source of power is removed by those who control the organizational environment, the rules of behavior will change, and the opportunity for a culture of genuine teamwork and energized collaboration will emerge.

I consistently come across this contradiction: businesses complain of silo behavior, yet they have systematically promoted those most likely to engage in territorialism. Current organizations are often seduced by the aggressive, the convinced and the decisive, but at what price? Surely, it is much better to harness these potential talents in a manner that can be channeled to support the whole organization, rather than just those of the fiefdoms. This will not happen as long as managers feel that they have no choice but to see their business world as an internally competitive arena where the quickest way to the top is climbing on the shoulders of their colleagues. Organizations will need to invest in those who truly commit beyond the boundaries under their own direct control and who genuinely sign up to the wider collective force. Recognition, financially and otherwise, needs to go to those who bring together and inspire, not those who divide and intimidate.

Of course, in the final analysis, it is the interworking of the three areas of Think, Feel and Know that matters most. Every organizational unit has a key role to play. If it does not, it should not exist. It is interesting to look to even the smaller 'mini-brains' in our bodies. The neurological unit responsible for respiration takes the airborne ingredients we need from the outside world to survive and thrive, primarily oxygen. The 'mini-brain' controlling blood circulation makes sure that the ingredients for ongoing health are distributed internally along the network of the blood supply system. In effect, the blood circulation system can be seen as a sophisticated motorway network. When flowing properly, the heart is more than capable of getting the right ingredients to the appropriate parts of the body to carry our repair and maintenance. This is the body operating in natural balance. The danger is the roadblocks and traumas that can limit the natural flows. How an organization senses and reports on natural flow and roadblocks is critical to its ongoing health. This requires active collaboration between Think and Feel reporting, with the 'big guns' of the brain and heart available to resolve difficulties only when necessary.

Organizational Design Principles

THINK STRUCTURE (INFORMATION)	CEO'S OFFICE (DIRECTION)	FEEL STRUCTURE (PEOPLE)
FINANCE	VISION	FACTORY
CUSTOMER	STRATEGY	DELIVERY
PROJECTS	POLICY	PRODUCT
PROCESS	DECISION AUTHORITY	SERVICE
TECHNICAL	RISK	
MARKET		
PEOPLE		

There is nothing about this proposition that is soft on performance. If people are developed in the right cultural environment, they will inspire and energize one another to higher levels of achievement. On the sporting field of team play, there is no hierarchy of significance, just a captain to make the occasional decision when necessary. The team want to perform to their best because they want to experience the energy of success, the feeling of personal and collective value and mutual commitment. They want to be viewed by their peers as excellent in their field of human endeavor. It is a natural human trait to want to create and to excel: this is where we thrive and push on the boundaries of who we really are. This is where we pursue the ultimate. Organizations who recognize this and work with this natural energetic flow will inevitably in time outperform those who work against it.

So, if not a blueprint for organizational success, I hope my observations and recommendations will trigger some useful debate. Of course, there has to be a realistic approach to transition, and each business would face some very critical considerations in terms of exactly how to translate these principles into a working structure and where to draw some of the lines of differentiation and collaboration. Yet, this should not be an excuse for procrastination. The need for change is screaming out loudly and clearly to all except those who choose to ignore it.

Section VI:

Summary

"Learn from yesterday, live for today, hope for tomorrow."

—Albert Einstein (1879-1955)

Over the course of this book I have attempted to bring alive the subject of neuroscience and demonstrate its relevance for everyday lives. Most of my experience is drawn from my business career, so the book is inevitably biased in this direction. Yet its relevance extends into all aspects of human behavior, relationships and performance. There is no better starting point than knowing ourselves, and I hope this has helped you to throw a little more light on your own thoughts, feelings and instincts.

It is an emerging science, with much left to teach us as our powers of discovery unfold. It is exciting in its power to reveal to us the dynamics of our behavioral choices and reactions. In this way, it spans all of life, and maybe even goes beyond it. I genuinely believe this can affect humanity's ultimate search for peace. When we strip away the complexities of the fears and behavioral choices that divide us, we are left with absolute unanimity in that which we all search for, the understanding and fulfillment of being human and the sharing of this experience with those we love and who love us.

Research and reading list: Think, Feel, Know and the underpinning science

Book/Source	Author/Works	Content
The Brain		
The Rough Guide to the Brain	**Barry J Gibb**	Brain physiology
Why Men Don't Listen and Women Can't Read Maps	**Allan Pease and Barbara Pease**	Gender differences
Human Instinct	**Lord Robert Winston**	Understanding instincts
Blink: The Power of Thinking Without Thinking	**Malcolm Gladwell**	The subconscious mind And 'thin-slicing'
Thinking, Fast and Slow	**Daniel Khaneman**	The fast and slow thinking brain
Neuropsychology for Coaches: Understanding the Basics	**Paul Brown and Virginia Brown**	Neuroscience
The Heart		
Heartmath Institute	**Company website**	Intro to neurocardiology
	Medical journals	
	Books	

Emotional Intelligence

Emotional Intelligence: Why It Can Matter More than IQ	**Daniel Goleman**	Introduction to emotional intelligence
Destructive Emotions: How can we overcome them?	**Daniel Goleman**	Further depth around emotional intelligence
Emotions Revealed: Understanding Faces and Feelings	**Paul Eckman**	Exploring instinctive and cultural behaviors

Others

The Power of Now: A Guide to Spiritual Enlightenment	**Eckhart Tolle**	New insights into human existence
A Child Called IT: One child's courage to survive	**Dave Peltzer**	Understanding human resilience in relation to extreme abuse

www.thinkfeelknow.com

Biography

Clive was born in 1954 in Blackwood, a town in the mining valleys of South Wales. After being educated at Pontllanfraith grammar school, he went on to study sociology at Warwick University.

He then emabarked on a corporate career, which started in human resources with Lucas Industries and Thorn EMI. He then switched into business management when he joined Ericsson: here he fulfillled a number of senior management roles, including chief operating officer for the UK fixed telephony division. He then spent some time in a change management role in London before becoming CEO of Pink Roccade UK, an IT business, which he ran for five years until 2005.

Since then Clive has returned exclusively to coaching. His main clients are people in business, typically business leaders in large corporate organizations, but also in smaller entrepreneurial businesses. He has also coached in professional sport and done occasional work in education, public services, charities, prisons and faith organizations.